Advanced Praise for *A Target on my Back*

"A legal thriller with a twist: A crazed lawyer and his wife, believing they have been wronged, become a modern-day Bonnie and Clyde and go on a terrifying murder spree. Next on their kill list is the new DA and her courage in confronting the killers makes this a fascinating read."

–Dennis L. Breo, co-author of *The Crime of the Century: Richard Speck and the Murders that Shocked a Nation*

"When murder comes to her town, Erleigh Wiley steps into the shoes of the slain district attorney and finds herself on the killer's hit list. In *A Target on My Back*, Wiley tells her personal story of overcoming fear in order to carry out her duty to hold Kaufman County, Texas together while the killer is brought to justice. Don't miss it!"

–Mike Farris, author of *A Death in the Islands: The Unwritten Law and the Last Trial of Clarence Darrow*

"Erleigh Wiley is one fearless prosecutor. She stepped up when called by the governor to serve as District Attorney knowing the danger— that a serial killer was stalking and killing prosecutors. This riveting first-person account tells the story of an unprecedented attack on the criminal justice system and how Erleigh Wiley provided steadfast leadership while being on the killer's hit list. Her courage in this deadly crisis inspired both Texas and the nation."

–Bill Wirskye, Second District Attorney for Colling County, Texas

"*A Target on my Back* is a unique first-person look into the world of crime-fighting in which the tables have been turned. The author takes the reader on an all-to real journey into what it means to stand for justice when your very life is in danger. A must-read!"

–Robert Kepple, Executive Director of the Texas District and County Attorneys Association

"*A Target on Back* captures Erleigh Wiley's journey as a judge then District Attorney in Kaufman County, Texas and the risks that all in law enforcement face every day of their lives."

–Robert Champion, retired Special Agent in Charge, ATF

"John Grisham and Scott Turow had better start looking over their shoulders for while Erleigh Wiley no doubt has a great legal-writing future ahead of her; she now has at least two career paths to consider. Wiley's engaging, nimble style immediately draws you into the action and proves that sometimes truth really is stranger than fiction. It's a good thing for us all that she lived to tell about it!"

–David Dean, Dallas attorney, former Texas Secretary of State and Chair of the North Texas Crime Commission

"A vivid first person account of living with danger and armed security twenty-four hours a day. Even more, it is a testimony to the extraordinary courage and dedication to the citizens of Kaufman County exhibited by Wiley in assuming the position of District Attorney."

–David A. Byrnes, Sheriff Kaufman County, retired; Captain Texas Rangers, retired.

A TARGET
ON MY BACK

A TARGET ON MY BACK

A Prosecutor's Terrifying Tale of Life on the Hit List

ERLEIGH N. WILEY

Skyhorse Publishing

Skyhorse Publishing books may be purchased in bulk at special discounts for sales promotion, corporate gifts, fund-raising, or educational purposes. Special editions can also be created to specifications. For details, contact the Special Sales Department, Skyhorse Publishing, 307 West 36th Street, 11th Floor, New York, NY 10018 or info@skyhorsepublishing.com.

Skyhorse® and Skyhorse Publishing® are registered trademarks of Skyhorse Publishing, Inc.®, a Delaware corporation.

Visit our website at www.skyhorsepublishing.com.

10 9 8 7 6 5 4 3 2 1

Library of Congress Cataloging-in-Publication Data is available on file.

Cover design by Rain Saukas
Cover photo credit: iStockphoto

Print ISBN: 978-1-5107-2170-8
Ebook ISBN: 978-1-5107-2171-5

Printed in the United States of America.

To my mother. My role model. She taught me to be fearless.
To the men in my life: my dad, my brothers, my sons, and my husband,
Aaron . . . thank you for being my life.

CONTENTS

| PART ONE |

Chapter 1
On Patrol

ON SATURDAY, MARCH 31, 2013, an old white Crown Victoria sedan methodically traveled along the pavement of farm-to-market road 987 just outside of Dallas in Kaufman, Texas. The driver knew the road well and had made the journey many times; the car's steering wheel moved surely through his hands, almost second nature. He surveyed the landscape, making certain nothing was out of the ordinary, checking to his right and to his left expertly. But he was being overly cautious—at this time on a weekend morning, before dawn, most commuters would not be leaving their homes for work and the cars were sparse. Leaving the city of Kaufman and moving into the unincorporated section of the county, the driver began to accelerate, merging onto 1641, another farm-to-market road. Still, no cars passed. It was peaceful, quiet, and still in the early morning darkness.

The driver had a companion in the passenger seat. Were they longtime friends or acquaintances sharing a ride? The two rode together in compatible silence, neither making conversation nor playing the radio as they drove along the roadway. Houses and businesses set along the roadside whizzed by. Few open spaces remained.

The driver turned off the main road onto Helms Trail, a growing area of Forney, one of several towns within Kaufman

County. Where there were once black dirt cotton-fields, homes seemed to have sprung from the ground as suburban sprawl reached Forney, Texas. Helms Trail is a narrow black-topped road that was one-lane in each direction; hard for a vehicle to pass alongside. Neighborhood streets forked off in each direction from the narrow lane, leading to more suburban homes. Helms Trail is usually a well-traveled road that carries homeowners back and forth to the busy interstates, but the driver passed no travelers at this early morning hour.

The driver continued to pass streets; he was no longer driving smoothly; he was accelerating. The car was speeding: 45, 50, 55 mph, although the road was marked 35 mph. What was his urgency? Then, a careening right turn on Blarney Stone Way, a neighborhood street scattered with houses. The car never slowed its speed until the driver pulled the Crown Victoria over on the side of the roadway near a house marked 9389 Blarney Stone Way. Before bringing the vehicle to a complete stop, the driver turned the car around in the roadway. The car never entered the driveway of the home, choosing instead to remain on the side of the road. The driver took a deep breath, opened the car door, and stepped onto the pavement, moving toward the front door of the house. The house was brick, with white trim. The house, a newer home not unlike the other homes in the neighborhood boasted one-to-two acre lots. Fastened on its front door was an Easter-themed wreath.

The companion stayed behind, moving over to the driver's side of the car. Exiting the car, the driver wore a cowboy hat low over his eyes, with his jacket clearly marked SHERIFF in bold letters across the back of his jacket, designating him as a sheriff deputy. He moved quickly to the front door, his AR-15, a lightweight assault rifle, strapped across his shoulder.

The knock at the door was urgent and loud; using the heel of his right fist to strike the door repeatedly. The homeowner looked through the peephole of the door. After seeing the deputy, the occupant cracked the door, and the sheriff pushed through. Then the slaughter began.

Chapter 2
In Chambers

POW-POW-POW. **WHAT WAS** that noise? Backfire from a passing car? I looked out of my office windows, which face the street that surrounds the courthouse square in the heart of Kaufman. It was 8:50 a.m. on Thursday, January 30, 2013, and car traffic was starting to pick up outside, as people hurried to the courthouse for their early morning court hearings. Cradling my first cup of coffee for the day, Richard Gadis, the Court Bailiff, stuck his head into my office, coffee in hand as well. I asked him to join me in my office, forgetting about the noise that I had just heard.

After our normal greetings, we started to discuss the trial that our Court had begun that week: the length of the trial, the number of parties involved, and other court observations. It was your typical morning at court for a judge and her staff.

Although that morning started out like many other ordinary ones, there was nothing ordinary about how I had become a judge in Kaufman County. My official title was Judge of County Court at Law in Kaufman County, Texas. The county court at law judgeship was a position that had been statutorily created by the Texas Legislature. I had been elected the first time more than ten years ago, in November 2002, but wasn't allowed to become the judge until the following year because of an election contest. My term was to begin on January 1, 2003, as every other elected official that won that year, but I began my term a year after my election, in November 2003.

I had won a hard-fought general election race in 2002. Before the election, Kaufman County was a Democratic-controlled county. In one general election night, however, my fellow Republicans and I turned the county red. Even though I was the winner of my race, the victory came at a cost.

Differing from every other Republican candidate who won office that night, I was the "first" in a two categories: the first African American countywide officeholder in Kaufman County and the first female County Court-at-Law Judge. Adding to that, my marital status, unbeknownst to me, was even more scandalous in the community. I was a divorced, single mom, with two sons under the age of seven. I had taken on a favorite Democratic candidate—one who enjoyed crossover support—and won. Perhaps not surprisingly, I had the smallest winning margin of all the other candidates on the ballot.

In fact, the *Dallas Morning News*, the largest paper in the metroplex, had called the race for my opponent on the eve of the election. Days after winning, I had a legal challenge to my office by my opponent, who was then given the enviable status of "holdover judge" by the county commissioners, even though he had not won the vote.

The Texas Constitution contains the holdover provision, which allows an incumbent officeholder to remain in their office until the position is filled. The judge I defeated remained in his position, receiving full salary and benefits, despite not winning the majority vote, for the duration of our legal challenge.

I was finally sworn in November 2003. By that time, I had raised and spent thousands of dollars to pay legal bills that arose from the court hearings, appeals, appeals of the appeals, briefs, and oral arguments in response to the legal challenge of my opponent.

Once the Court of Appeals ruled, deciding the legal matters in the case, the political issues took care of themselves. The Commissioner's Court, who conducts the general business of the county, acted quickly, acknowledged my winning votes by canvassing the 2002 vote totals for my race and swearing me in as the new Judge. Legally, the Court of Appeals decided that my opponent who was defeated had no standing to challenge the election results; politically, the commissioners wanted to put the rightfully elected judge on the bench. I earned it and the people of Kaufman County must have agreed: they reelected me in two consecutive unopposed election terms.

While elections could be complicated, my job as judge was straightforward. Judges had rules to follow. My job was to be unbiased, to listen to the facts and apply the law.

But as that January day in 2013 unfolded, I was reminded that doing what was right didn't always rule the day and that a wrongdoer wouldn't care about the facts, or the law. They lived by their own rules, by their own laws.

REFLECTING ON HOW I became judge was in the past, and I kept those long-ago thoughts to myself as Richard and I shared a compatible silence. As we sipped our coffee, my thoughts returned to the present. We wondered aloud if we could possibly finish the trial this week. The case in question was a Child Protective Services (CPS) case. Child Protective Services a state agency that is designated to protect children who are abused and neglected. If the abusers are the parents, the State may ultimately ask a jury or a judge to terminate the parents' rights to their children if the parents can't protect their children. The evidence in these sorts of cases is generally brutal and emotional, and this one was no exception.

In fact, this case was more challenging than most. The number of parties and their conflicting interests were complicated. There were five parties involved: the mother, two fathers, a grandparent, an attorney ad litem for the two children, court-appointed special advocates (CASAs) and five attorneys that represented the five parties. While I sat on the bench and listened to the evidence, I had created a flowchart and diagrammed all the players to keep everyone's names straight as we proceeded with the evidence.

But in a moment, everything changed. A case that was so important quickly lost my attention for the rest of the week.

The events of the morning were a kaleidoscope; a quick movement caught my attention out the window of my office. The windows covered one wall of my office, in the Hopper style of windows, opening from the top of the pane with the glass opening into the room. I turned the latch and opened the window, ready to yell out into the melee. Then I recognized another one of our sheriff deputies. I saw Deputy Ragsdale, one of the court bailiffs, moving fast. He was a retired cop who worked for the Kaufman County Sheriff's Department and was a bailiff for another Court, the 422nd District Court. Court baliffs were deputy sheriffs who were assigned to individual courts to protect the judges when court was in session. Many court baliffs were retired police officers.

Deputy Ragsdale was moving as fast as his age and health would allow. Besides his quick movements, my attention was drawn to the look on his face. His facial features were different; gone was his usual jovial expression, replaced with a set jaw that exuded tension.

Richard and I looked at each other. He sprang into action, handing me his cup of coffee. Richard got on his hand-held radio, which crackled with static. No one answered his calls. Something was wrong.

Richard walked back through my offices, past my two staff members, and headed toward the outside door to the hallway. As he walked through the glass door, he called back over his shoulder.

"I will be back," he said. "When I know something . . ." His voice trailed off, as he quickly headed out the door and into the fray.

It wasn't even nine in the morning.

"MAN DOWN! MAN down!" someone shouted.

Are gunshots what I heard earlier!? My mind was questioning and rebelling at the same time. *This couldn't be happening.*

I opened my office window again and stuck my head out, trying to understand what was being said through the commotion that had started outside. All the noise came from the southeast side of the courthouse square along the sidewalk, which was adjacent to the public parking area.

I leaned farther out the window, with the thought of yelling at one of the many law enforcement officers that seemed to have sprung up from the sidewalk. Only moments ago, there was no one outside, except for Deputy Ragsdale. Before I could open my mouth, someone from the shouted at me.

"Shut the window!" the voice adamantly yelled. "it's not safe."

Quickly obeying, I snapped the window shut and quickly latched it. My thoughts were jumbled. *What was going on?* My mind reeled.

I walked out of my inner chambers into the outer office, where my staff was seated. Their faces said it all.

"Judge, I think someone shot Mark . . . Mark Hasse," Katie said. "One of the deputies just told us." Katie was my court administrative assistant or court coordinator, the brains of the court operations. A court coordinator was the term used within the court system to describe the judge's administrative assistant.

Kim, a part-time employee, nodded in agreement. "I thought I heard something popping, like a distant loud noise," Kim said. "I didn't think it was gunshots. I'm trying to call Warren."

Warren was her husband, an experienced Dallas police officer. His experience did us no good that day, however, because no one could reach anyone. The phone lines were overloaded.

Finally, word reached our office and to our worst fear. Finally, word reached our office and confirmed to our worst fear. There had been a shooting. Mark was down.

* * *

MY MIND WAS reeling. I had heard those same distant noises before in another courthouse, in a different county ten years before.

In 1993, I was involved in a shooting at the George Allen Sr. Courts Building in Dallas, Texas. The George Allen Courts Building at that time housed all the remaining courts that hadn't moved in 1990 when the Dallas County Commissioners finished construction on a law enforcement center across the Trinity River. The George Allen Courts in 1993 was teeming with family, juvenile and civil court judges, which occupied more than thirty courts in an outdated building. Then, I was an Assistant District Attorney in Dallas, prosecuting cases in the trenches. I had just started a new assignment in the Juvenile and CPS Division and I was learning the ropes in that department.

The day of the shooting, I was in the court coordinator's office when I heard loud noises.

BOOM!

Did someone knock over a file cabinet? I thought.

Then another: *BOOM!*

Finally: *BOOM!*

That was no file cabinet. That was a gun discharging, I finally realized.

I still remember the people who were in the room with me as the gun went off. That day, we became battle buddies, bound forever by a tragedy cloaked in gun smoke and fear: Tom Nelson and Donna Winfield, two private attorneys, and Dorothy Corley, the court coordinator for Judge Gaither. Our eyes were huge; our mouths dropped open.

Dorothy got on the phone to call the police. The phone lines were jammed. (In 1993, cell phones weren't ubiquitous like they are today.) The three of us huddled in the corner. Donna opted to crouch under Dorothy's desk, as we huddled over her using the office phone. We called and called and got nothing but a busy signal.

We heard distant screaming. Then, *BANG!*

Something or someone pounded the door. We looked at each other.

"Is it the shooter?" we whispered. Whoever it was, he or she was trying to get into this office.

As one body, we moved en masse to the door. We must have looked ridiculous but fear does strange things.

Poor Tom—as the only man, we huddled behind him as we shouldered the door, blocking entry. Forget women's lib. His shoulders were broader. We had determined that we were safer with the intruder on the opposite side of the office door and we held our ground at the door.

After a few minutes, the noise from the other side subsided. We breathed a sigh of relief. We cracked the door open after a few minutes and saw bloodstains smeared across the hallway's linoleum floor. We panicked, slamming the door shut in a hurry. That's the exact moment I learned that fear could actually make you physically ill. I was sick to my stomach. *Why was there blood down the hallway?* Then we heard more screaming and scurrying of feet in the adjacent courtroom. *Oh my God, what was happening?!*

Dorothy got back on the phone to try and place a call, and this time, we got through. There had been many phone calls, we were told. We were assured by the 911 dispatcher that the police were on their way, and so we sat there waiting for the police to arrive, huddled together and praying.

Later, we learned that an estranged husband had come to court to respond to a protective order involving his wife and children. A protective order is a civil court order issued to prevent continuing acts or threats of violence. The abuser wanted his family back and he didn't agree with the judge that had entered the temporary protective order against him. He approached his wife in the hallway, but she said she was done. And so he pulled the trigger.

The rest of our questions were quickly answered. His first shot missed her shot missed her, ricocheted off the hard floor, and hit a teenager standing nearby, who had been waiting for his hearing in Juvenile Court. The irate abuser next shot his wife fatally and then turned the gun on himself. The pounding at the door was the juvenile in question trying to find safety, while we barred his entry into the court coordinator's office. The screaming in the courtroom came from citizens, witnesses, and litigants who fearfully witnessed the scene at hand. The running noises originated with those same people, all of whom were running away from the doors at the back of the courtroom to the relative safety at the front of the courtroom behind the Judge's bench. They too had been frightened by the young injured juvenile, as he searched for safety, banging on the courtroom door.

On the noon news, Judge Hal Gaither of the 304th Juvenile Courts demanded safety measures at our courthouse, similar to what was in place at the criminal courts. Safety requirements changed that day for all courthouses in Dallas County.

That was ten years ago in Dallas, and now a shooting had happened in Kaufman county. Similarly, I was officed in an antiquated courthouse, with few safety measures for the staff and community that moved in and out of the courthouse.

I WASN'T AN attorney as in 1993, I was the judge, and on that day it was time to enter my own courtroom and let the parties, litigants, and particularly the Assistant District Attorneys (ADAs) know that one of their own had been shot. I opened the door and realized there was no one to announce my entry. Normally, my entrance into court was announced with an "All rise, Kaufman County Court at Law is now in session, the Honorable Erleigh Norville Wiley presiding." Today, every bailiff was busy outside of the courtrooms, securing the courthouse.

No one was coming in and no one was going out of this building.

I cleared my throat. Up until that moment, I didn't know that a lump had started to form. Once I opened the door, most attorneys rose out of respect and habit for the Court. Once I stood on the bench, all eyes turned, fixing themselves on me. I didn't take my seat, so everyone remained standing.

"I'm sorry to announce . . . that . . . there has been a shooting here at the courthouse or actually right outside of the courthouse," I said. "I think it happened out toward the parking area." I pointed in that direction, and then turned to face the district attorneys in my courtroom.

"Mark Hasse was shot," I continued. "We've been instructed that no one can leave the building for security reasons. I'd ask everyone to remain at the courthouse and probably here in this courtroom, except for the ADAs. I'm sure you want to go upstairs and to your offices. We are awaiting more news. The court is in recess until 9:30."

I exited down the stairs of my court, went through my chambers and outer offices, and entered the jury room. Although it is generally not allowed for anyone but the bailiff to have contact with the jury, I thought today's event called for an exception.

I knocked on the door, entered, and repeated the same instructions I had given to the parties inside the courtroom. By the look on the jurors' faces, they had already suspected something else was going on besides the usual court delays. Then I departed, shutting the door, and leaned my head on the outside of the jury door.

"Judge, you okay?" asked Katie, coming up behind me.

Her eyes were brimming and she choked back tears as she continued, "We were just talking to Mark last night when we left Diversion Court." Diversion Court was an additional court that I had after hours. It was a proven way to redirect drug- and alcoholic-dependent nonviolent criminals with additional court time, therapy, and a team approach instead of the traditional punishment court model.

We hugged. We had worked together so long that we often shared the same thoughts. Right now, we both felt guilty. Last night at the end of a long work day and an additional court docket, Mark was talking to Katie and me in his usual nonstop way. Mark had been a prosecutor for years. He had a war story for every situation and he liked to share them with anyone that would listen.

I never worked with Mark when I was a Dallas ADA. He had already left the office when I was hired by the then elected district attorney, John Vance, in 1990. At that time, Mark was in private practice representing criminal defendants. I may have had an occasional plea with him, but I was a misdemeanor prosecutor at that time, handling minor-level criminal offenses. Mark would have been handling more serious felony cases. A misdemeanor plea would have been an agreement entered into by the prosecutor and defense attorney, which wouldn't have been memorable since it is such a common practice in the daily disposition of criminal matters.

Once Mark became a Kaufman County ADA, he would come by occasionally to talk to my court staff, or I would see him in my court, training younger prosecutors. He had returned to prosecution, his first love when he was hired in Kaufman County in 2009. If you were alone with him, he liked to talk about all the bad dudes (this included both men and women) that he had prosecuted from back in his Dallas glory days. When I spoke with him, he would regale me with stories of days past, as well as some current ones, if the cases weren't in my court. Because the worst of the many bad guys he had prosecuted were sent to the penitentiary, he was especially conscious of safety and always said he was packing a gun. I believed him.

Lately, whenever he saw us, Mark flirted with Katie, while regaling us both with a new war story; last night was no exception. He saw us and was going to launch into another noteworthy war story. It was already a late night and we were not in the mood, so we made our excuses and ducked into the ladies' room to escape a lengthy diatribe.

But now, we both felt guilty.

"Katie, we didn't know last night," I said. "We were tired. Have you—"

My sentence broke off as Richard opened the outside glass door to my office. Katie and I had been standing in front of the jury door, in the entrance to my office. We had to back into the office, so the opening door wouldn't hit us.

"Mark Hasse is dead," Richard said. "He was assassinated."

We spoke in unison.

"Who did it? Why? What happened? . . . Oh my God!"

Richard shook his head. His face indicated there were no answers, although we all had a singular thought of who hated Mark, but it was still unspeakable. The person that hated Mark was one of us.

That's the last time I saw Richard that day.

Chapter 3
Computers, Pay Sheets, and Videotapes

"**BABY** . . . baby! Erleigh! I have been trying to reach you. What's going on out there? How are you?"

It was my husband, Aaron, calling my work phone. The landlines were not jammed anymore. I glanced at my cell phone—it was working as well. In fact, it was blowing up with text messages from concerned friends and family. Obviously, the news of the shootings had gone viral.

"Aaron, I'm fine," I said.

"Someone just asked me how you were," he said. "I didn't know what they were talking about. You didn't call. What the hell is going on out there? Where are you?"

His tone was a jumble of worry, frustration, and a little anger.

"I'm fine," I said. "Obviously, I'm in my office. You are talking to me on my work phone. There was a shooting—"

"I got that," he said, cutting me short. "That's why people were asking me how you were!"

I kept talking.

"It was Mark . . . Mark Hasse," I stammered. Conveying what happened was harder that I had anticipated. "Aaron, he's dead . . . Someone killed Mark Hasse."

"It's Eric Williams," he fumed. "Someone needs to dust Eric Williams's hands for GSR right now. I knew it. He is crazy mad. He is furious about the prosecution of the theft case and anyone else that has ever gotten in his way. You've got to start carrying a gun. He is coming after you!" I knew that he meant a GSR examination, which was a criminal investigative tool. The acronym stood for gunshot residue. It is the residue deposited on the hands of someone who discharges a firearm.

I rolled my eyes. We had had this conversation before.

"I agree with you . . . that he might have a motive to kill Mark," I said. "I think Eric is suspect number one, but there's no way he is looking for me."

I heard his sigh, but I rushed on.

"I think Eric is suspect number one," I repeated. "But I don't know what's going on. I'm locked in the courthouse."

"That's probably smart, safe," he said. "No one in. No one out."

"That's what Richard said," I told him.

That seemed liked a lifetime ago. It had probably only been twenty minutes.

"Listen, I will call you back on my cell," I said. "I took a thirty-minute recess. I'm going back into court. I'm sure the DAs know now and I need to get the jury dismissed for the day."

He sounded totally aggravated.

"I want to see you," he said. "I don't give a shit about that jury and I don't want you anywhere near Kaufman right now!"

"You sound ridiculous," I said, my tone changing. "I've got to take care of the jury and get things wrapped up here. I can't just leave."

"No one is doing a trial or anything else today," Aaron said, confirming the details. "A prosecutor just got shot fifty yards from the courthouse."

"I know, baby," I said, relaxing my tone. "But I gotta get things squared away here before I get to you."

"I love you," Aaron said, his voice softening. "Call me when things settle down. I've got my cell. Things are kinda crazy around here too."

"I love you back," I countered.

"Stay away from that crazy Eric Williams," Aaron said as we ended the conversation. "You know he hates you."

"JUDGE WILEY, I would like you to take over CPS," Judge Chitty requested. It was 2007 and we were having a judge's meeting. The Presiding Judge, Howard Tygrett, had initiated these periodic meetings for the judges to discuss different issues that would arise. The presiding judge had the unique distinction of being manager of court operations and would decide which cases the other judges would be assigned to hear.

Tygrett urged, "I would like to make that assignment if you are willing to accept it. The CPS billing is out of hand and you have prior CPS experience in Dallas County."

Judge Chitty earnestly looked at me with his bespectacled eyes.

"I know you are as busy as we are with our dockets, but these attorneys . . . Well, particular attorneys are billing the county quite a bit and there has been a lot of talk and the commissioners are starting to question the billing. Since you've had the experience, it could be easier for you to review the billing."

I nodded in acceptance, internally thinking, *Well, I asked for this. Now I've got it.*

I felt I had more varied court dockets than the other judges. Court dockets are the title given to the summary of proceeding in a court of law. My court had extra-jurisdictional authority for a county court, which gave me more power and authority than the average county court. It made for exciting work, but it also increased my caseload volume. This would be an additional assignment, but I had been telling the judges at other meetings that I had the experience if they needed help. Now they were asking for my help.

"Sure, I will be glad to take a look at it and see what I can do." I answered aloud.

I knew it would never go back to the other judges. I also knew what an assignment meant; I was not only taking on reviewing the pay sheets, but all the CPS case responsibilities. That meant handling attorneys' appeals of the associate judge's rulings, signing Emergency Removal Orders, and covering hearings if the associate judge had a scheduling conflict. This was going to be more than just paperwork. In CPS court, the cases involved the most serious of family cases: where the state has taken custody of children and removed them from the offending parents.

I knew I would need help. And I knew just the right person to help me with this transition: Angela Webb. Angela was my former Court Coordinator. She was the consummate professional and was efficient at her job. She only left my employ after seeking a higher position as the District Clerk, which is an elected position.

After the Judge's meeting, I approached her with the Court's new assignment.

"Angela, as the CPS bills come in—if the pay request from the attorney is over a thousand dollars, I want you to pull the court file from the District Clerk's Office and we are going to review the attorney's bill request individually, comparing the bill to the court file," I said. "If the billing is under a thousand dollars, I will review the billing and unless something stands out, I will sign and send my order to the auditor for payment to the attorney. On the bills over a thousand dollars, I want you to review the billing first. If there are any pay vouchers that are inconsistent from the documents in the file, give them to me and we will discuss the discrepancies."

Angela was nodding along with me, making quick notes on her legal pad.

I always liked that about Angela, She never wavered from a task. In fact, she liked investigating and special assignments. The day-to-day grind wore on her, like it did on us all, but luckily, I had Katie Griffin, our newest hire, that Angela was training. Angela now had time to dig through the pay sheets with me as we tried to determine why the CPS billing was increasing exponentially in our county, while the caseload was not. It didn't make financial sense.

Aloud I said, "I think we will be able to notice a pattern pretty quickly."

"Do you want me to pull the pay sheets that have already been signed by the other judges and submitted to the auditor to see if there have been any discrepancies?" she inquired.

Always wanting to do more. I admired that.

"No, what's done is done," I said. "That was at the other judge's discretion, I don't even want to get into that. We will start with the new pay sheets that the district judges are asking me to sign and review and then move forward."

I gestured a forward motion with my hands.

"Clean slate. Make sure you float my new assignment to the attorneys, as they are turning in their pay sheets. Let them know that I am reviewing them for discrepancies. They won't like it, but it gives them an opportunity to correct any mistakes on their pay sheets. And don't comment if after you share my new policies, they don't want to turn them in or say they may have made a mistake, as long as they correct them."

Angela winked. She understood. She had finesse.

"I've got it, Judge."

The male defense attorneys loved her. She was a beautiful red-head, with a figure to match. If anyone could get them to cooperate, she could. Her outward appearance was half a match for her brains and personality. Angela was clever and learned quickly and she played the Southern belle with ease. She loved to drop endearing Southern expressions that had become outdated, but sounded charming from her. When she went to the movies, she described the outing as "going to the picture show." When she went to the bathroom, she would toss a parting expression, "I've got to powder my nose."

I TEXTED AARON, Don't forget to let the kids know.

I didn't want them to hear about the shootings from one of their friends and think that I wasn't safe.

He responded, "Going to court. Will handle when I return." Classic Aaron: brief and to the point.

It was close to 10 a.m. It was time to reenter the courtroom. This time when I opened the door, to enter onto the bench, an attorney announced, "All Rise."

Everyone was standing. The prosecutors were back from the District Attorney's Office, their faces stained with tears. They might have been in shock or at least a state of disbelief. From their faces, it was certain that they knew Mark had been killed.

I started to speak, but that lump was unexpectantly back in my throat. I was forced to pause, and gather myself. I cleared my throat, but my eyes filled with tears.

Carol Wilson, an attorney retained to represent the grandparents in the case, spoke up.

"Judge would you lead us in prayer, pray for Mark and his family?"

My first thought was, *I'm Catholic. We don't pray spontaneously and certainly not aloud.*

I looked down at my court reporter, Scott Smith. Scott was just an all-around good guy. He was my court reporter and he pastored a small church on the weekend. He could pray, but I looked back at Carol and she gave me a reassuring nod, like, *This needs to come from you. You are in charge in this courtroom. We need you.*

So I prayed. Even to my ears, it sounded strong and I knew it was sincere.

"Dear Heavenly Father, help us today as we . . . as we try to understand how one of our own could be gunned down and to remember that even in this, you are in charge, even now. Pray, Father, for Mark. Pray for his soul, as he joins you today. Help console us as we mourn his loss and we try to understand the unimaginable."

I was wracking my brain.

Did he have a family? I think he had a sibling, a brother or sister, but for the life of me, I couldn't remember which. He did still have his mother.

"Pray for his mother, Lord, that she will be able to find peace even in this tragedy. In your name we pray, Lord."

I then started the Lord's Prayer and those in the courtroom joined in. We ended the prayer in the Protestant way.

"For thine is the Kingdom, and the Power, and the Glory, for ever and ever. Amen."

The rest of that Thursday morning sped by. Jurors and witnesses were escorted to their vehicles by either sheriff's deputies or other peace officers that had swarmed the courthouse. The jurors' cars were parked in the same parking lot as the shooting, which had now become a crime scene. As they walked to their vehicles, some jurors cried while others looked away from where Mark's blood had stained the parking lot asphalt.

My staff confirmed the jurors' cell phone information and we agreed to contact them tomorrow for an update about Monday. I had already decided there was not going to be court the next day, a Friday.

I sent my staff home and sped to meet Aaron in Forney, which is the town where we live. We decided to meet at a local restaurant we knew away from Kaufman and this horrible crime scene. It was well past noon. I still wasn't hungry, but my husband and I just wanted to meet, we needed to see each other, to assure ourselves of our own personal safety, and to begin to sort through one of the craziest days of our lives.

When I arrived, Aaron was staring into a drink. It looked like he hadn't touched it. I sat down next to him. We just held each other for a couple of long minutes.

We decided to turn our cells off, so we could finish our sentences without interruption. Since the shooting, our phones were buzzing, ringing, and being generally annoying. Everyone was well intentioned, but we were worn out. We would return calls later.

We had one eye on each other and the other on the TV over the restaurant bar. We had already contacted our family and Aaron had reached out to the staff at both our sons' schools. Jacob's school allowed him to talk to Aaron over the the phone, but he had to go by my eldest son's school. The school secretary wouldn't remove Brad from class to take the phone call. It was school policy, but this wasn't something you could reduce to a written message over the phone and have a school attendant deliver a note to your kid between classes. Brad was the older of the two boys and a senior in high school. Imagine being eighteen years old and hearing, I don't know if you've heard, but there was a shooting at the Kaufman County courthouse. Your mom wasn't shot, but a District Attorney was. Don't be late for dinner. Not a good idea.

From that day, some things have been forever changed.

"Poor Brad," Aaron started, his eyes welling up. "He was really upset. He had no idea about the shooting, but he said when I showed up at the school for no reason it freaked him out."

"This is so crazy," I said. "It's still hard to believe."

Aaron stood firm.

"Eric is the shooter," he said. Before leaving the courthouse, I had been briefed by Richard. Aaron wasn't the only one that had thought Eric was a suspect. Deputies had gone out to Eric's residence and found him in a shoulder sling when he answered the door. When questioned about his whereabouts this morning, he acted surprised and said he was recovering from shoulder surgery. He consented to having his fingers dusted for gunpowder residue.

It was a good try by law enforcement, but the witnesses at the scene described the assailants as masked; and that the shooter wore gloves.

Despite Aaron's certainty, I wasn't as convinced: "I'm just saying, why would he kill Mark over that theft case? I'm sure he hates him, but Eric is a lawyer, a former JP, or Justice of the Peace. Killing someone is a lot." A justice of the peace is a judicial officer of a lower court who is elected. They handle smaller civil disputes and criminal matters. It is job holding the honorary title of judge.

"It's a lot for normal people, for reasonable people," he said. "He isn't either. He is a sociopath. Eric can't get beyond the fact that Mark took him on. Mark Hasse's hard work led to his conviction. The craziest thing is Williams probably doesn't even understand why he had to give up his bench."

ERIC HAD BEEN charged with theft of property. It is difficult to understand why Eric would have committed theft, when he could have purchased the items he stole. Why would an attorney and an elected Justice of the Peace steal computer equipment?

Eric's version of the facts was that he wasn't stealing anything. He claimed that the county had not provided the necessary computer equipment to enable him to do his job and he was going to take monitors home and put together the system he needed for work and then bring it back.

This is a standard criminal's story. In reciting this, Eric sounded like the stereotypical shoplifter, who tells him- or herself, "I forgot

I had the item in my purse" as he or she passes the last checkout line in the store. Given the opportunity, every thief would return the goods or money they "accidentally" stole, if given the chance. Any epiphany comes only after they get caught, of course.

And just like the shoplifter with the stolen items tucked into their purse or pockets, Eric's "smoking gun" was a video capturing his theft of county property. The video showed him sneaking around the offices of his colleagues, unaware that the Sheriff's Department had placed some additional security cameras in the building. No honest employee sneaks around after hours, ducking around areas they think are under surveillance, secreting county equipment for lawful purposes. More importantly, when a county official or employee wants to request a new computer for their office, they request the necessary county computer equipment through the Internet Technology Staff, commonly referred to as IT. Once approved through your budget, the IT department delivers your county computer equipment. It is tagged and inventoried to your department. These are standard procedures to protect taxpayer dollars.

His actions on the video were way past the last checkout.

In 2012, the Texas Judicial Commission had reviewed the video and suspended him without pay or benefits. They entered findings that Eric was in violation of several judicial canons. For Eric, that was the death knell. Only later did I learn that as a result of his suspension, his COBRA—the insurance plan he used while the case was pending—was terminated. After Mark went to court, a jury found him guilty of theft. Eric was removed from office. This was a devastating blow, as Eric and his wife both suffered from chronic illnesses: diabetes and rheumatoid arthritis. He received notice of the termination of his health benefits the week before he killed Mark Hasse.

ERIC HAD ONLY decided to run for JP once his attorney ad litem work that he performed through CPS become minimal. Eric resented me because I stopped him from overbilling Kaufman County for legal work he didn't do on CPS cases. Prior to my Court taking on the assignment, he had been billing more freely with minimal oversight. Eric's billing had escalated and had amassed close to half a million dollars over a three-year period.

When he got caught on the theft case, Eric had many options of what to with his criminal case. After the evidence of the videotape emerged, everyone felt that Eric would make the best plea deal he could get. Rumors circulated that the District Attorney's Office sought to remove him from his position as JP. At one point he was offered a decent plea deal: plead to a misdemeanor theft, with a deferred probation period and in exchange, resign from the JP bench. With a deferred probation, which meant no final conviction, he could have kept his law license. The actual value of the computer equipment stolen was a felony-level offense. A felony meant automatic removal from office and a serious problem with a lawyer keeping his law license. The DA's offer of a misdemeanor was more than reasonable. Eric didn't take the plea offer.

Eric had so many stops along the way before it got to murder. Initially, he could have taken the plea if he would have agreed. In Texas, trials are a two-part process: guilt/innocence and then punishment. After the conviction in the first phase of the trial, seeing that the jury didn't believe his innocence, he could have tried to strike a deal for punishment with the prosecutors. Maybe he could have still been able to practice law, to make a living and have a life.

He could have moved on from the justice of the peace court. He could have moved away from Kaufman County and started anew somewhere else, somewhere no one knew him or his wife. Instead, he decided he had nothing to live for and nothing to lose. Or maybe he thought no one was going to tell him what to do. Who will ever know what he really thought?

But if I had to guess, I believe that Eric thought that he was beyond the law. He had to think he deserved the job as the Justice of the Peace in spite of everything that had happened. He wouldn't accept a guilty plea; the evidence against him didn't matter. He deserved it, all of it. The money he hadn't earned, the computer equipment he hadn't properly requested, and now Mark's life.

If Eric killed Mark there was no doubt that Eric blamed Mark and wanted to permanently remove him. Was I one of those people he thought was standing in the way of something he deserved? My husband thought so. I hadn't considered it then, I just thought—I was just doing my job.

But now, I wasn't thinking about me and how I felt. I was thinking about all the things that had happened today. Aaron grabbed my hand and squeezed it hard. We looked at each other.

The lump was back in my throat and I couldn't clear my throat without the unshed emotion finally being released. This time the tears streamed down. I cried for Mark, who was forever lost.

Chapter 4
Man on Fire

MIKE MCLELLAND DIDN'T have the usual prosecutorial background for a high-ranking law enforcement official. Many of those elected as Criminal District Attorneys began their legal experience in another District Attorney's office as an Assistant District Attorney, where they amassed their trial skills and figurative "skins on the wall." When you started as a new hire in a Criminal District Attorney's office, you wanted to be a trial attorney and ultimately wanted to litigate serious criminal cases in front of a jury. To get there, a new prosecutor would be assigned traffic offenses, then move to misdemeanor assaults and driving while intoxicated offenses. If you continued your career as a prosecutor you would be assigned more serious cases—felony offenses and then violent felony offenses. It wasn't uncommon to have been involved in twenty jury trials your first year as an entry-level prosecutor. Unlike most of the rest, Mike's strength didn't lie in his courtroom skills, but his administration. He had run his own private law firm and had served in the military. He was also very social, as Mike and his wife, Cynthia, were known for their ready hospitality. They liked to entertain, and entertain they did. They hosted parties for the District Attorney's office and for other elected officials. They opened their home for an annual Christmas party, which included their family, friends, and other colleagues. Cynthia was also known to enjoy baking for her husband's staff, and Mike delivered goodies weekly to the DA's office. For the office staff, starting their young families, when new babies were expected, Mommy Cynthia usually had a baby blanket in the offing. Mike was known more for being a "nice guy" than for his prosecutorial prowess. However, when Mark was killed in the streets of Kaufman, just steps from the courthouse, he changed forever.

Mark had been hired by the previous District Attorney in 2010, but when Mike was elected and came on board as the new Criminal District Attorney, Mike and Mark became fast friends. Upon learning of Mark's murder, Mike was devastated. Seemingly overnight, he evolved from an easygoing man to a man on a mission to avenge his friend's murder. I listened to Mike at the press conference after Mark was shot. He was no longer affable Mike; instead he was a man on fire.

Mike had been elected as Kaufman County's DA in November 2010 in his second bid for the office. During the first bid, he ran against the former District Attorney Rick Harrison in 2006, and Rick barely eked out a victory in that election. Rick Harrison was a big presence—when he entered a room, you knew it. He was a guy's guy, a natural storyteller who knew everything about everything, especially when it came to sports. (I think he secretly would have chosen being a sports announcer for college football games on Saturday afternoons over the daily grind of practicing law.) But nevertheless, he had mastered the practice of law. We had worked together in the Dallas District Attorney's Office in the '90s and Rick left the DA's office in Dallas and managed a successful criminal defense practice in two counties.

Personally and professionally, Rick had done well. He had married into a local political family and inherited his love for law enforcement from his dad, a former FBI agent. As a former Dallas

County prosecutor and a successful defense attorney, he had legal prowess in his own right.

Although Rick's biting wit could be annoying at times, no one could take away the fact that he had brought Kaufman County into the twenty-first century in terms of law enforcement. Rick had many accomplishments, but his most noteworthy was co-founding a local Children's Advocacy Center in Kaufman County. It quickly became a place where children could safely go and report their abuse and neglect to trained interviewers, and then receive therapy services. After some personal issues, Harrison ran again, but was defeated. It was no secret that Mike gained from Rick's private mistakes. The two men effectively switched positions. Rick went back into private practice and Mike took over the helm of the Kaufman County Criminal District Attorney's office in January 2011. It was a tough pill for Harrison's friends to swallow, but no county could have a District Attorney with Rick's mistakes and look the other way at the ballot box.

Mike came into office under Rick's shadow, but with Mark still there (one of Rick Harrison's last hires and a career prosecutor), the office had talented prosecution and a Criminal District Attorney that wouldn't morally disappoint.

Once in office, Mike accomplished some difficult tasks as the District Attorney in his three years: prosecuting county personnel, specifically a high-ranking employee in the County Tax Assessor's Office for theft; taking on a bad gun law that protected gun ranges at the expense of property owners, passed by the State Legislature; and finally convicting a Justice of the Peace for stealing county computer equipment. I'm sure Mike felt proud of his record and planned to glide into reelection, unopposed, with a sure win.

When Hasse was killed, Mike expressed his opinion that Eric Williams was Mark Hasse's murderer, both privately and publicly. Mike's adamant public discourse could have put the bulls-eye on his back next. Later, we learned that Williams did have a hit list.

Did Mike's opinion about Mark's murderer move him to the top of Eric's hit list? Or was he always the next target because he approved the prosecution of Eric and partnered with Mark during the prosecution of the theft case against Eric?

Case in point? Mark's memorial service took place at the courthouse. The Monday after Mark's murder, Mike arranged a memorial service to honor Mark on the front lawn of the courthouse. It was a solemn occasion that drew hundreds, including Kaufman County employees, community members, and the press.

Mark had been a certified peace officer, as well as an attorney, and he deserved all the pomp and circumstance the occasion required. He was a prosecutor for the state of Texas, struck down for doing his job. We stood with our hands over our hearts, as the flag was lowered to half-mast to signify the loss of our fallen colleague.

Mike was the master of ceremonies and spoke at the service. Mike's rousing statements at the ceremony left me stunned: he clearly issued a challenge to Mark's killer. It was similar to his remarks at the press conference. He wanted to be clear, anytime he was presented with an opportunity, to let the killer or killers know: we are coming to get you.

The word was out in the law enforcement community that Mike felt Eric Williams was the killer, but the initial police investigation was veering away from that theory. The Kaufman Police Department was the lead investigating agency, as the crime occurred in the city of Kaufman. Kaufman County District Attorney's investigators were keeping close tabs on the case. Because of this, there seemed to be some level of distrust between the Kaufman County Criminal District Attorney's Office and the other members of law enforcement. The DA investigators felt that the investigation was not focused on the right suspect and the DAs wanted to investigate and protect their own.

Still, Mike made it clear in his speech during the memorial that he wanted Williams to know he was coming after him. He never used Eric's name, but he spoke directly to the killer and we all knew he believed that the killer was Eric Williams. Did Eric feel that he was issuing a challenge directly to him?

Mike said, "We will find out who killed Mark Hasse and that wherever you . . . whatever rat hole . . . that you are hiding in . . . we are going to pull you out of it and you are going to be found and that justice will rain down on you." Mike's words were powerful and unwavering.

When the memorial ended, we in the crowd wiped our eyes and silently filed back into the courthouse. It was the beginning of a work week and I still had a jury trial from the previous week to finish. We had been in recess since Thursday because of the murders.

To this day, I greatly respect the jurors in this case: they all returned the following Monday to complete their service and they attended the memorial service before court began, under the watchful eye of the Court Bailiff. After entering the courthouse, we filed into my courtroom and began the work at hand.

And that is how it went for me for the next few months. One day, another week, weekends flying by with the kids. My oldest son's senior year in high school, my younger son adjusting to a new school.

It wasn't long before it was Valentine's Day. Spring Break. Family ski trip. Easter weekend was approaching fast.

Everything was back to normal. We stopped speaking about Hasse's death. Information leaked from the crime scene: maybe it was a girlfriend, or the lack of a girlfriend, tax problems, an old case he prosecuted. No one really knew.

We had nothing.

But Mike always said he had the answer. Unfortunately, no one was listening to him.

Chapter 5
Who Killed Mark Hasse?

LOOKING BACK, THE weeks following Mark's death were marked by two distinct ongoing occurrences. The first was the County's reaction to the death of Mark Hasse, which remembered and honored the life and loss of the slain Assistant District Attorney. The second, of equal importance, was the ongoing investigation into his murder.

Legally, the prosecution doesn't have to prove motive in a murder case. But human curiosity inevitably asks why. Why was this murder committed?

Of course, the crime scene investigators were processing the evidence at the parking lot, Mark's home, and his District Attorney's office files in Kaufman and Dallas Counties for possible clues. Was there a person that Mark had prosecuted in the past that had recently been released from the penitentiary?

However, those efforts yielded little fruit. There was so much contradictory evidence. For instance, several witnesses did see the shooting, yet eyewitnesses at the scene reported similar, yet markedly different things. One fact in their stories remained constant: the shooter was masked, making it hard to identify him or her.

Similarly, investigators' search of Mark's home did not turn up many clues. It wasn't atypical to investigate a murder victim's personal life for a possible murder motive. But there wasn't much to go on. Mark had been a single, older, confirmed bachelor and except for a few peccadilloes, there was no real motive for murder. The trail at his home and personal life had run cold.

The investigation kept coming back to his work as a prosecutor. Who had he pissed off enough that he or she would want him dead? That could be an exhaustive list. Before his death, Hasse had earned a reputation for being a hard-nosed prosecutor.

The better question was this: Who would act on it? Who had the nerve to pull off the murder in broad daylight, in the courthouse parking lot, with dozens of police in the area patrolling and standing yards away inside and outside the courthouse, as they parked their patrol vehicles?

I think one of the benefits the murderer had in eluding authorities at the time of the shooting was that Mark had prosecuted so many cases in Dallas and Kaufman County that it was hard to zero in on a specific suspect. Then, three coincidental events, essentially red herrings, occurred that played into the killer's favor, moving the investigation away from Eric Williams as a suspect.

First, the Justice Department released a press statement on the day of Mark's shooting thanking all the different partnering agencies that assisted in an Aryan Brotherhood investigation, which led to the criminal prosecutions of numerous members of a local Aryan Brotherhood gang. Mark and the Kaufman County Criminal District Attorney's office were among the named agencies recognizing them for their assistance in the prosecution of AB gang members. It wasn't unusual in a large federal investigation to have several local law enforcement agencies involved in major cases. After the conclusion of one of these types of cases, the federal agency issued press releases summarizing the investigation, explaining the outcome of the prosecution, and thanking local authorities.

Red herring number one.

Second, there had been a Colorado prison warden killed by a Colorado prison warden killed by a white supremacist group two months after after Mark's murder, by someone who pulled off his nefarious act disguised as a pizza deliveryman. The prison warden's murderer traveled to a county near Dallas and was killed and was killed in a fiery shootout, with the charred pizza delivery costume in the backseat. Investigators asked what seemed like obvious questions: Why was he in Texas? Was he part of some conspiracy to kill law enforcement? Was this yet another white supremacist murder, Mark's being the first? Mike McLelland was not persuaded about these suspects and Mark's murder, but other law enforcement officials thought there may have been an evil connection.

Red herring number two.

Third, there had been Mexican cartel activities on the border, which heightened Texas law makers sentiment regarding Mexican gangs and the killing of government officials.

There had been an example of a Mexican cartel-style shooting had been a "Mexican cartel"-style shooting two counties over, two months later. The shootout occurred in the midst of an upscale north Texas community: an attorney was shot to death in his vehicle. This was an unprecedented attack this far north of the Mexican border. Had the cartel moved this far north and was Mark's murder one of their first attempts, followed up by the killing of an unarmed attorney? Though the time line didn't fit, it didn't matter because it conveniently played into the theory of Mexican gang violence north of the border.

Red herring number three.

This trifecta of events led investigators down a rabbit hole of false leads and wasted time. Many theories abounded as a result.

One was that the Aryan Brotherhood decided to go on the offensive and take the fight to law enforcement, which would have been highly unusual. The Aryan Brotherhood's strength lies within the penitentiary system, but if they were the culprits, were the Colorado warden's murder and Hasse's murder connected? Were Kaufman County and our local law enforcement team targets of a larger conspiracy?

The AB did do murder-for-hire hits, but it was almost always against one of their own, usually for some perceived wrong or for snitching to the cops. So this didn't fit their profile. It was also interfering with their low-level criminal activity; because of the investigation, police were all over the Aryan Brotherhood in northeast Texas. They were questioning AB in prison and out. Aryan Brotherhood wouldn't want this much "heat" on them. It wasn't good for business. It was hard to promote illegal gambling, run prostitution, and sell drugs with police officers questioning members at every turn.

Another theory was that all the violence and chaos that comes with life south of the Mexican border had moved to the Dallas-Fort Worth area. Had the Mexican drug dealers decided they wanted the DFW area? Were they going to start picking off prosecutors like in Mexico to send a signal to law enforcement? Was it an attempt to chill the rule of law?

It all sounds highly improbable, thinking back on it now.

But during the investigation in the early months of 2013, anything was possible. Every theory needed to be chased down and investigated. And in that eagerness to turn over every stone, to vet every semi-viable lead, Eric was able to stay in the shadows.

He emerged only when he reached an internal boiling point: He just couldn't stand Mike's mouth and he had to shut him up. Permanently. If he hadn't needed to kill Mike—and this makes me shudder—he might have gotten away with Mark's murder. He could have gotten away scot-free . . . and continued down his hit list.

| PART TWO |

Chapter 6
Cocktails, Chaos, and Murder

"**I CAN'T DECIDE** what I'm going to have to drink," I said. My mood was light-hearted. It had been two months since Mark had been killed on the streets of Kaufman; although there was no suspect in custody, the community was returning to normal.

I was teasing our hosts and good friends, Rick and Sandra Wilson. Rick had already poured a generous portion of red wine into my glass.

"I think you'll like this," he said, with a knowing smile.

The Wilsons were amateur wine connoisseurs. Our first introduction to the California wine country had been with them. They were self-made business owners. They married young and worked shoulder to shoulder. Sharing their home, plane, or wine was always fun. They were generous hosts and had been our friends since Aaron and I moved into the neighborhood in 2004, and our friendship had grown over the last decade. We occasionally traveled together, and frequently shared dinners out, discussing our mutual concerns, which sometimes were politics, but mostly concerned our children and their grandchildren.

That night, we had been invited to a dinner party at the Wilsons' home. Their backyard beckoned summer; it was March 30. The night was beautiful. There was a light breeze, with no humidity. Spring on a Texas evening could be perfect and that night it was. Although it was still too cold to swim, the pool and the fountains bubbled in the background and lent to the Wilsons' home the restful ambiance of a resort.

Conversation flowed around me as I sipped the Syrah Rick had graciously offered. There were three other couples in addition to myself and Aaron, as well as Sandra's dad and my aunt. The grill sizzled as Rick prepared steaks to order. There was the happy chatter of friends and family as our conversations filled the air, with contemporary country music playing in the distance.

"This is your call," Aaron said, as he handed me his cell phone that he had scooped out of his pocket. "It's Katie. She wouldn't be calling me."

Then I heard the grumble under his breath.

"She never has her cell on her," he snorted. "It's always somewhere else."

"I heard that," I said, as I grabbed his cell out of his hand.

My phone was in my purse. I had chunked my bag in a chair on the way out to the patio hours ago and I hadn't thought about it since.

I felt a little guilty. A police agency was probably looking for me to sign a search warrant (crime didn't take a break) and had called Katie, my court coordinator, when they couldn't reach me.

"Hey, girl. Sorry I didn't have my phone. I left it in my purse and . . ." I started, but I stammered.

I recognized Katie's voice, but not what she was saying.

All I could make out through the blur of words was, "Judge . . . Judge."

She was sobbing. I couldn't understand her. The first thing I thought was that her stepdad had a heart attack. He had had some recent heart problems. But what she said next really confused me.

"Are you alright!?" she asked. "It's Mike."

"What? Mike who?" I asked.

"It's Mike McLelland," she said. "He has been killed at his home and they are looking for you and Aaron to make sure you are safe."

Katie was scared—really scared—and this is a lady that doesn't frighten easily.

"I couldn't reach you on your phone and I started, then I started thinking . . ." She interrupted herself. "I got scared for you when you wouldn't answer your cell phone."

My expression must have changed dramatically. The party atmosphere had evaporated and the dinner party guests were all looking at me. Sitting closest to me was Aaron.

"What is it?" he demanded insistently.

I repeated Katie's words aloud, both for him and the other guests' benefit. I was also trying to wrap my mind around what she was saying and what it meant.

"Mike McLelland was killed tonight," I said.

Everyone in the backyard gasped.

"Where was he?" I asked Katie.

I repeated her answer out loud, "At home."

"Where was Cynthia?"

I repeated her answer.

"She was at home. She was murdered, too. Oh my God!" Katie started crying anew.

I looked at Aaron in disbelief. I handed him his phone.

My hostess collapsed in a lounger and wept. We all knew Cynthia and Mike McLelland. These weren't strangers. These were our friends and colleagues. It was hard to believe. And for a moment, it was hard for me to wrap my brain around what I had just conveyed to my friends—that the Kaufman County Criminal District Attorney and his wife were murdered in their home on Easter weekend.

I looked at Aaron and I knew what he was thinking: Eric had struck again and he had to be caught before his evil visited our home.

From that point on, that night was a blur.

As if the tragedy wasn't enough, we were still parents. As we began to take our leave from the Wilsons' dinner party, our sixteen-year-old son called us.

The good news? He wasn't drinking. The bad news? He got caught holding beers for kids at a Dallas club for under twenty-one-year-olds. After passing the portable breath test with a score of zero, the officer called us and we were instructed to pick him up.

Probably got caught just before he was going to start drinking, I thought.

When Aaron and I picked him up, he had no idea that my silence wasn't solely about considering his punishment. I was still mulling over the night's events and the vicious murder of the McLellands. And because of that I was actually too spent to be angry. I couldn't have imagined that this evening would end this way. It was late and we went to bed both mentally and physically exhausted.

We had to go to church the next day. It was Easter. It was an unusual Sunday and Easter celebration for our family.

By now, it was clear that Saturday night was a tragedy of historic proportions. No two District Attorneys from one office had ever been killed in our state's history.

It begged the question: Was the true target all county government officials in Kaufman? Was it just the District Attorney's office? Were they going after the government in general? Was it a grievous attack against the state of Texas or Kaufman County? Was it the Aryan Brotherhood? No one knew for sure.

And because of that uncertainty, my life changed.

Chapter 7
Do I Have Your Attention Yet?

THE FOLLOWING MONDAY, some of the elected officials gathered for a meeting in the County Judge's offices. The judge's office had become a central meeting place at the courthouse for the elected official. Included among the group were myself and the three other court judges, the County Judge, and the sheriff. From time to time, others joined us. We sat around the conference table in the Judge's chambers.

The men seated with me had never had to plan the succession of a state official being assassinated in his of her own home. Frankly, I don't know of many counties that would have anticipated plans for such an event. If an elected official is unable to perform the responsibilities of their office, an interim District Attorney would have to be designated until there was time for the governor to make an appointment. In this case, Mike McLelland was permanently unavailable. Even the sheriff, a retired Texas Ranger with illustrious credentials that included "cleaning up" the Branch Davidian debacle in Waco, looked unsure. The siege in Waco, which is located almost a hundred miles south of Kaufman, happened in 1993 when our current sheriff was a Ranger Captain and at the behest of Federal prosecutors in Texas; the Rangers were asked to take charge of the crime scene after the conflagration and to collect evidence from the compound.

Oh, shit, this is not going well, I thought. *We all thought it was Eric Williams, but how can we prove it?*

We were talking to one another. We also had our phones on the table and were nervously checking them from time to time. Our spouses, family, and friends were constantly calling and texting, worried for us.

We were also checking in and being checked on by senior level attorneys from the District Attorney's office. They were assisting in implementing the next course of action. The governor's office called, as well. We reassured the governor's office that we would swear in an interim DA. We hoped to swear in the First Assistant, if she would accept the temporary job.

As the elected officials and judges who worked with the DA's office, we had asked the entire District Attorney's office to meet us in one of the courtrooms. We somberly walked into the courtroom. They DA's office had already gathered. When I saw those young attorneys, investigators, and support staff, it was hard to check my emotions.

All but one prosecutor was gathered in the courtroom with the judges and the Sheriff, seemingly awaiting instructions and an update. The office wanted to help find the killer of their boss and coworker.

As their faces streamed with tears, the judges and I all spoke to them. I remember giving them praise.

"I know this is unprecedented, but I appreciate your service," I said, the words catching. "The fact that you are here and that you came to work . . . speaks volumes. I promise you we will take care of you and that you will all be safe."

I hoped I could keep that promise. I had no idea how, but we were going to find the killer. We had to find the killer.

I walked back from the courtroom and stopped by my offices to check on my staff. Court had been cancelled for the day, but my staff came to work anyway. Understandably, they were pretty badly shaken, too. Somehow we felt safer at the courthouse together than apart at our homes.

It was still hard to believe that two additional people, both connected to the Kaufman County DA's office, had been killed. We were now dealing with a serial killer.

As I entered my office, a group of men waited there to greet me. A couple of the men wore suits that just screamed government official. Another one looked like he was from the government, as well, but he was dressed more casually.

"Judge, we were just coming to speak to you about your security," one man said, extending his hand. "We've met before. I'm Maurquis Fromby, with the US Marshal's Office. I think you know my boss, Earl Jeffers."

My brain was reeling. I remembered meeting him before, but what were these three guys doing here talking to me about security?

Granted, the past weekend had been pretty scary. We had the local police and the state troopers at our home over the weekend, keeping watch at night while we slept, which I thought was going to continue for a few more days.

These guys looked a lot more professional, more serious. Maybe that should have been a relief.

But it scared me even more. I was wondering if they had a new, actionable threat.

Two men followed me into my chambers and one stayed behind in the small waiting room, watching the door as I faced the two agents, Marshal Fromby, whom I had met before, and another agent I did not know. The agent I didn't know extended his hand and introduced himself as John Garrison. He was part of the US Immigration and Customs Enforcement, otherwise known as ICE. It is a subdivision of the Department of Homeland Security.

"Judge, we are here to protect you," John said. "Our office will take your security detail. We will have three eight-hour shifts. On this detail, my people will be with you for twenty-one days and then we will reevaluate."

I know my face must have looked incredulous. My mind was still trying to determine if something new had happened that required the assignment of these federal agents.

"Do we have your cooperation?" he asked me. "We can't protect you without your cooperation or that of your family."

"Agent—" I faltered. My mind was trying to remember the name of the agent I was speaking to. "Of course, I will cooperate."

I gulped my nervous energy down as Garrison handed me a document to sign. The lawyer and judge in me are embarrassed to admit that I didn't even read what he put in front of me. I assumed it was probably some agreement to spy on me.

My world was starting to tilt.

He stood up. I noticed he was speaking about me to Marshal Fromby, but not to me.

"I'm going to contact the tech team," he told Fromby. "We will have a truck at the Judge's house at 1700 hours and get everything set up by nightfall. Sheriff is already ready to go."

I wondered how did he know where my house was and what was going on at the sheriff's house?

He finished our brief interview by looking at me and extending his hand.

"Thank you, Judge," he said. "We will take care of you."

Fromby thanked him as well, they shook hands, and Fromby stayed behind to continue my briefing. When the agent left, I collapsed back in my chair.

"What the hell is going on?" I demanded. "Has something happened?"

Marquis spoke to me as if I was a petulant child.

"Judge, nothing else has to happen," he said. "We have had two District Attorneys killed within two months of each other, plus one's spouse. We have orders that this is a high priority and we are going to keep you safe." When he said orders, he motioned up. Orders from higher up the chain, Washington, I presumed.

He looked at me and then he glanced at my open window blinds in my office facing the street. He stood up and clicked the blinds shut.

"Are you trying to get killed?" he asked. "Don't you realize that there could be a sniper on the roof, or someone driving by and shoot you through the window?"

By now, my mouth was in an "O" shape. I felt near tears. Marquis must have sensed my feelings because he pulled back a bit.

"Judge, until we know who killed these people and why, we are not taking anything for granted."

He stopped and let me gather myself.

I'm not a little kid, I thought. *I'm the Judge and my safety is important because if something else happens, it would create an even greater crisis in this county, maybe even this state. Oh God, maybe the country!*

Now that he had my attention, he explained the threat assessment and some safety tips. He also told me Homeland Security was going to have to set up at my home to protect my family for at least the next three weeks. It could be longer. We wouldn't know for twenty-one days. Later I learned that the Sheriff had instructed the federal agent that I was a priority.

After he left, my head was spinning. I had so many conflicting thoughts. *Am I an idiot to stay at this job? I mean, this is just a job. I could quit. Would it matter for my personal safety if I was still in this job? Is this someone hunting the DAs or is it specific individuals they want? Is it Eric?*

Once the thoughts started, I couldn't stop them from racing around in my mind. *But everyone thinks it is Aryan Brotherhood. Either way, I'm screwed. If it's Eric, Aaron thinks he hates me. I don't know anymore. Does he hate me enough to kill me? If it's AB, I'm it. I'm the only black person elected countywide and I'm a Judge.*

The ringing of the phone shook me out of my reverie. It was Aaron

"Baby, been talking to some folks around here," Aaron said. "We've got Homeland!"

I snapped at him.

"You almost sound gleeful!" I fumed. "This is ridiculous."

"I'm not happy about any of this," he said. "Our lives have changed and we are in danger. Eric will kill you—"

I cut him off. I couldn't figure out why him stating what I was thinking about Eric irrated me. Probably because maybe he had been right all along.

"Stop. Stop!" I said, forcefully. "I'm really trying to think here."

"Calm down," he said, his tone softening. "I'm not trying to upset you. Whoever killed the DAs may kill you. He, or she, or they are still out there and if we have to have a security detail, I'd rather it be someone top-notch like Homeland. I work with these guys. They want to help. I'm only afraid about what happens if we don't find the killer and we lose our security detail in twenty-one days."

His voice trailed off.

"You're right," I said. "I'm sorry. I'm jumpy. Marquis From—"

"Fromby," Aaron said, finishing my sentence. "Good guy. Was he down there?"

"Yes, and he scared the crap out of me," I confirmed. "Snapped my blinds shut. He talked about a sniper shooting me through my windows. These guys are way over the top."

"Earl trained him," my husband assured me. "He is good people. The US Marshals do security for the federal judges here in the Northern District. They are good."

Earl Jeffers and his wife, Rosalind, were good friends of ours. When I met her ten years ago, she was a second-career new lawyer, working in Kaufman County as an Assistant District Attorney. Rosalind had come into my chambers with her usual aplomb and stated I was going to be her mentor while she was an ADA in Kaufman County. Ten years ago, Earl was a wild-eyed US Marshal, breaking down doors. Now, she was the dean of students at a law school and he had been promoted to supervisor with the US Marshals. Earl and my husband also shared the same kidney disease and had transplants within a year of each other.

"Okay, I'm glad then," I said, smiling. "Are you happy?"

"I will be happy when they catch this sicko," he said.

"Aaron, stop," I told him. I wanted him to stop talking because I thought he was going to launch into more about Eric. Sometimes talking about the murderous events set my teeth on edge. Particularly with a new security detail outside my doorway. "I'm heading home. I've got some guys waiting outside my office I need to meet—they're ICE agents. They are ready to head over to the house to see what the tech guys are setting up, whatever that means. By the way, how do they know where we live?"

"They are the federal government." I heard the smile in his voice. "See you at the house. I love you, baby."

His voice has always been able to melt me, even when I'm mad. His voice has a quality that is soft and sexy, and it gets me every time.

"Love you back."

After we hung up, I wrapped things up at the office and took the first of many trips home with a security detail in tow. The evening shift had two vehicles, with three agents apiece. One car was the lead, the other car brought up the rear, and I drove in between the two vehicles.

Once I arrived at my house, I realized that what Marquis had explained about the security at my home was nothing like I had imagined in my mind. It was like a scene from a movie.

The unfortunate part? I was the star in this movie of life.

There were guys on the roof, putting some type of device in my chimney. There were men knocking on neighbors' doors to inform them that we were setting up infrared parameters alongside my neighbors' property. Men were checking locks on the gates, adding additional cameras, sticking wires in the ground. Local cops were coming by to meet the Feds so they could familiarize themselves with each other.

I wondered how the local police knew the Feds were at my home.

My neighbors were out in their yards, looking on. I wasn't surprised—nothing this exciting had happened in our neighborhood, ever.

My neighbor across the street, Veronica, walked over when I got out of the car with two vehicles in tow, holding her squirming toddler in her arms. She was trying to remain calm, but it was clear to see that she was upset. As a neighbor, she was one of the best, always keeping a watchful eye out.

"I didn't see you or Aaron or the boys and these guys showed up," she explained. "Well, I called the police."

That explains why the police are here, I thought.

"Well, then they showed me their credentials," she continued, her eyes getting huge and welling with tears. "They are Federal agents. Are y'all safe? Are we safe?"

She clutched Cash, her two-year old son, closer.

"They are keeping us safe," I said, as I hugged her. "You guys are fine. I'm so sorry."

In that moment, I realized the impact of what was happening in my life, to me, and now to my neighbors.

"This is just a precaution," I assured her. "I promise." This was the second time that day I had promised to keep someone safe, and the day wasn't even over yet.

I looked her squarely in the eyes, squeezing her free hand, and we both turned and looked at the organized chaos, as men hurried around the yard and throughout the neighborhood, moving quickly and efficiently. This wasn't the first time that had to set up a safety parameter around someone home.

"Judge! Judge Wiley!" one of the agents called. "We would prefer if you would stay in your car until we approach the car and get you out. It would probably be better for you to pull into the garage and not just park here in the driveway."

The look on my face must have been one of shock.

"I was just talking to my neighbor—"

"And we are just trying to keep you safe," he interrupted, gently. "Can we go in? Thank you, Judge."

Oh my God. I'm a prisoner in my own home.

Once I got inside, I tried to act normal in my own home, as strange but well-meaning men and women set up their staging room in my formal dining room. I overheard them say it was the best room because they had access to the front door, could see the back door, and were close to the garage door. They were trying to cover all exits.

I was relieved when I heard the roar of Aaron's car, since it meant that he was home. While my husband doesn't have many vices, he sure does like his sports cars. He drove a Z06 Corvette. The sound of the motor usually informed me of his arrival before he did. I was in our bedroom and hurried back through the house, where the agents were setting up, toward the garage door, to greet him when he walked in.

"Hey, baby—" I stopped. He was shaking hands with the agents in the dining room.

"Hey, baby," he responded. He had a big grin on his face. "I know all these guys. This—"

"They've already introduced themselves," I interrupted.

I don't know why I was annoyed. Maybe because he knew the security guys, and he looked so comfortable while I was so uncomfortable. Or maybe because he somehow knew this day might come and I didn't see it coming.

I went back into our bedroom. As I walked away, I could hear them talking about cases that they had done together; war stories from the federal criminal court system.

"What's up with you?" Aaron said, as he entered our bedroom about fifteen minutes later and closed the door.

I was sitting on the chaise. He came over and hugged me.

"These are good guys," he continued. "They know what they're doing. They are professional and they are going to keep us safe. I'm glad."

"Well, I can tell that," I said, my tone laced with sarcasm. "You're in there shooting the breeze, having fun."

"Listen, I'm not enjoying having people in our home any more than you, but until we get the killer arrested, I'll sleep better and not worry when I'm not with you," he said.

He stopped and really looked at me.

"You do realize there is a killer on the loose?" he said. "I wouldn't be surprised if he is looking to kill you next."

"You are so dramatic," I shot back, getting angrier by the second. "Do you say things like that to scare the hell out of me or what?"

"I'm not just saying things to scare you or to be mean," he responded. "I believe it. I believe the killer is Eric and he wants to kill you. Until this case breaks, we aren't safe. You aren't safe."

We had covered this ground before. Aaron's theory was simple: I was the beginning of Eric Williams's end. When I had confronted him in 2008 about overbilling the county for legal services, Eric stubbornly took himself off the list of court-appointed attorneys that do legal work for indigent clients in CPS cases, a mainstay of his legal practice. He lost thousands of dollars. His practice began to fail, but then he rebounded. He ran for office and won in 2009, becoming the elected Justice of the Peace in Kaufman, Texas, in 2010.

However, when Eric was charged, indicted, and tried in 2012 for theft charges, he lost his position as JP. The Texas Judicial Conduct Board suspended him without pay from his justice court bench; and later, the State Bar of Texas did the same with his law license. His refusal to accept a misdemeanor plea offer had vast adverse consequences on his career and livelihood.

Eric blamed me for stopping the county pilfering; but he hated Mark Hasse more. Hasse had dared to try him for a crime that in his warped mind Eric did not believe he committed. Even if he did something wrong, Eric felt he should be able to return the county property and pretend it never happened. Isn't that the way it used to happen in the ol' boys club of Kaufman County? Those days were gone, if they ever existed.

Then there was Mike. Had Mike propelled himself into Eric's path when he called Eric out at a press conference and the memorial service for Mark, or was Mike next since it was his office that spearheaded William's prosecution? Mike was speaking directly to Eric and Eric knew it, and I believe he hated him for it.

My husband believed that in Eric's mind, he wouldn't have had any of these problems if a certain nosy, black, female judge in Kaufman County had stayed out of his business. I use to think that Aaron's theory was wild and farfetched. I didn't know anymore.

My husband hugged me.

"I know," I said. "I now believe it's probably Eric, too. But I don't think he would kill me."

My stubborn nature would not let me concede the unspeakable. Still, I squeezed him back.

"You stood up to him," Aaron said, pushing me gently away so he could look into my face. "You don't even get it. Eric was doing what he wanted and you said no. A black woman told him no. After all, Eric is a strange white guy. I don't know about his background, but there is something about him and race that doesn't add up."

He hugged me again. We both got up off the chaise. I started taking off my work clothes and donning sweats. I had to convince Aaron to take his work clothes off and get comfortable. He was at home and the agents didn't expect him to remain in his suit, even though they had a professional relationship with him. As an

Assistant United States Attorney with the Department of Justice, he handled many ICE cases.

I began to wonder if I was just being stubborn about Eric. The evidence pointed to him as a person who had a grudge against Mark Hasse and Mike McLelland, but could he have brutally killed Cynthia, someone who was only tangentially related to this whole mess? Did he want to kill me? Would my family be the casualties of his vendetta, too?

That night, it started to sink in, that the previously unthinkable was my new reality; somebody wanted me dead and would go to great lengths to make sure that it happened.

Chapter 8
Why Not DA?

LIFE CAME AT me fast over next few days.

I set aside some of my usual judicial responsibilities to deal with the Herculean task of dealing with the new duties that had arisen since Mike's death. The group of elected officials that had met the Monday after Cynthia and Mike's murders reconvened to discuss some of these issues. We knew that the sheriff was now leading the investigation. Mike and Cynthia lived in an unincorporated area of the county, which invoked the sheriff's jurisdiction. The sheriff's jurisdiction encompassed the courthouse and the unincorporated areas of the county. A retired Texas Ranger, Sheriff Byrnes had credibility, but the enormity of these murders had every law enforcement agency—local, county, state, and federal—involved.

The governor's office contacted the county and indicated that the appointment process would proceed normally in Austin, but they wanted the County to let the governor's office know if the County had any preferences or if there were any issues that we might make them aware of as the process moved forward. The governor's office usually made these inquiries through their own appointment staff, but everything was being fast-tracked, and they wanted to have all bases covered. This was not a time for politics. They were going to still do their due diligence, but wanted to make sure that the county officials provided any information about the appointment applicants as soon as possible.

Brandi Fernandez, Mike's first ADA, had accepted the position as interim District Attorney already. Texas law allows for this when vacancies occur, but only for twenty-one days. The clock was ticking on the governor's appointment. He and his staff had to work within the timeline imposed by outside events, plus the governor's office expressed that they wanted the right person for the job for the County, particularly in light of these horrific events.

Judge Wood, the County Judge, had asked the other judges to meet with him in his office. We had met about three times during the week and he wanted to update us on the different applicants. We sat around Judge Wood's conference table, contemplating the candidates. We had learned that Dennis Jones and Taryn Davis, two strong possible applicants, had decided to decline seeking the appointment and did not want to be considered. There were still two capable candidates to recommend: Casey Blair, who would later be elected District Judge in Kaufman County, and Brandi Fernandez, the acting DA.

Still, the consensus around the table was that it would be better to give the governor's office more than two applicants. So we discussed other options, tossing about names of other applicants that we might approach about applying. The concern was not merely seeking qualified attorneys: we sought someone with a Kaufman County connection who could keep the citizens calm; someone who would send a strong message that there was a capable person at the helm. It was understandable that the climate in Kaufman County had risen to a near panic, and the county needed someone strong to lead during this turbulent time.

Looking back, there was a real sense of urgency because there were three dead people and the body count was potentially rising. Even more alarming, two District Attorneys were among the dead.

None of us wanted our local community to think we governed a lawless county. So, candidates with deep community roots seemed an asset, as well as their legal abilities for this appointment.

Judge Tygrett cleared his throat. "Judge Wiley," he said. "You should do it."

"I should do what?" I questioned.

"You should be the DA," he said, rushing on. "You've been an assistant district attorney in Dallas County. You've been a judge and you're from here. You grew up here in Kaufman . . . I think."

I cut him off.

"Well, Judge, I didn't think you wanted me killed that badly," I half-jokingly responded.

Judge Tygrett and I had always had an awkward, sometimes tense relationship. While he was the senior-most judge in age and experience on the bench, I often thought his joking manner and his need to be liked sometimes diminished his judicial persona. I knew he had intelligence to spare, but he spent a lot of time trying to manipulate situations. I preferred the straightforward approach.

As he revealed this newest brainchild, I thought it might have been an attempt to get me out of his way. There were no political secrets in this county; during the previous election (2010), I assured him that I would not run against him for the District Judge position and he indicated that he would not seek a fourth term. He planned to enjoy his golden years with his wife Linda. Unfortunately, as a lot of constituents discover with their candidates, election-season promises are rarely kept.

He liked being a judge. But if I took his advice and accepted the appointment as DA, it would make his broken promise to step down a little more palatable. I could already hear the spin: "Well, since Judge Wiley decided to accept the appointment, there was no clear other qualified person that could run for my bench," he'd say. "So, I am going to seek a fourth term."

"Erleigh," he said, interrupting my reverie and changing his tactics. "I really think that you would be the best person for the job. The solution is right in front of us."

He looked to the other Judges and Sheriff, who had joined us after the interviews.

"Judge," Tygrett hesitated.

I looked into the eyes of Judge Mike Chitty, who presided over the other district court. I considered him to be unbiased.

"It goes without saying that you are the most qualified for this job in every way, but I don't know if you want it," he said, holding my gaze. His eyes misted a little bit and the gravity of Judge Tygrett's suggestion hit us all.

It was unspoken. We all knew danger was involved.

The last DA was dead and we did not have the killer in custody. Judge Chitty's nerves were stretched thin. He was the judge that presided over the theft case, of which Eric was found guilty. It was not illogical to think he might be next, since he had sentenced Eric.

I glanced around the room and the other judges were nodding in agreement with Judge Chitty. I looked at Sheriff David Byrnes and he looked squarely back at me.

His expression said it all: **no**.

Sheriff Byrnes was the same man who had helped me win my first election. He had rolled up his sleeves on election night, more than ten years earlier. We had a great friendship and mutual respect for one another.

I hated what these murders had done to him. He was seventy, but his flat stomach and broad shoulders typically gave him the youthful appearance of a man twenty years younger. But lately his face had begun to show the strain of this case. He was carrying the investigation, the safety of all the county officials, and the community on his back.

"You guys are really serious," I said, clearing my throat. "I hadn't thought about it really. I think I should excuse myself now that my name has been thrown in, and not be a part of any more conversations or discussions . . . I think it would not be appropriate." I faltered, "Excuse me."

"So, are you thinking about it?" Judge Wood asked.

"I guess I am," I said, as I stood up and left the room.

"ARE YOU NUTS?!" my friend Kim asked.

Kim Walker's voice bordered on hysterics, as she explained how she felt about my suggestion of being Kaufman County's next District Attorney. I had not been able to reach Aaron and needed to talk to someone. After the meeting I had puttered around my office, but could not focus on any of the legal briefs, motions, or orders on my desk and decided to go home and think through the new turn of events.

Me, the next DA . . . I thought.

Kim was a confidante with no connections in politics, particularly Kaufman County politics. Our friendship had begun as parents. Our children went to the same schools and shared many of the same events and activities, which is how we met. I thought an outsider's opinion would be different. It was different all right.

"Are you kidding?" she asked. "Your black butt would be the target of those KKK motherfuckers!"

"They're AB," I said, feebly.

"You know what I mean," she countered. "You've got a perfectly good job. You're a judge. I'm not a lawyer, but isn't that a step down? More work. More headaches! I see no advantages."

She overwhelmed me, and made me think I was crazy for even considering this career move.

"Someone has to do it," I said evenly.

"Let some of those white folks do it in Kaufman," she countered.

"It's my county," I said, tearing up. "My mother's birth certificate is in that courthouse. She was born here. I'm not just going to let them gun down people on the streets of Kaufman like it's the flipping Wild, Wild West."

"Girl, I hear you," Kim said, softening her tone. "I get you. I know you're a Republican and I don't always get that, but you need to really think about this. People are dead. They are really dead. I don't want you to be next."

"I know," I said, much more calmly as well. Our voices having dropped a few decibels, we were finally talking in normal tones.

"I love you," she said. "I will pray for you. I will support whatever decision you make. Talk to Aaron."

We hung up. Tears ran down my cheeks.

Was I nuts? Would the AB see this as a chance to kill a black female DA and make some real headlines? But didn't Eric do these murders and we couldn't prove it yet?

It was circular. I was going in circles.

Chapter 9
It's More Than Just a Mere Detail

DESPITE LIVING UNDER armed guard, the other responsibilities in my household had not stopped. Mine is a busy, blended family. I have two sons, Jacob and Brad, from a previous marriage, whom Aaron and I are raising together. We both also have busy, high-stress legal jobs.

But I never fully appreciated how busy our lives were until those agents shone a spotlight on us. They made me realize that our lifestyle was more than busy—it was nonstop.

In fact, because of the way that I lived, my detail had already given me a nickname: "Traveler." I think I earned that moniker after I inadvertently lost the country's finest as they followed me to work one morning.

To explain, getting up and getting to work in 2013 started with driving my youngest son, a high school sophomore, to Bishop Dunne Catholic School in Dallas. That drive was forty minutes from my house and about an hour back to Kaufman.

He had to be dropped off by eight in the morning. That meant I had to leave my house by a certain time to miss the school buses in my neighborhood and the heavy traffic of commuters that were travelling from the suburbs. I wouldn't say I was always speeding, but driving aggressively was part of the route negotiation.

I took the "country cut-through" to avoid a longer roadway. A "country cut-through" is a road that isn't usually on a mapped route, but the locals know it and save time by utilizing it.

However, the guys in the detail didn't have the roadway on their mapped route to Bishop Dunne. I had no idea until I arrived at Dunne that I might have lost my detail and they were not just hanging back on the drive over.

After that little snafu, I was encouraged not to drive my car.

My detail decided that in order to protect me, I had to be in their car. I still think that they were a little embarrassed that they lost me. I thought it was humorous and no harm done.

They did not. Their sense of humor was different than mine. This was their job and I was their responsibility. They took the implied threats against the elected officials in Kaufman County seriously and no one wanted to lose a potential target on their shift.

What they did not fully appreciate was that my life at the time of the shooting was more than my job as a Kaufman County Judge. In fact, the detail would have preferred it if that had been the extent of my responsibilities. I think they breathed a sigh of relief between the hours of 9 a.m. and 5 p.m., hours when I wasn't on the move. However, my real work began before nine and ended well after five.

They couldn't believe my schedule.

After getting Jacob to school, I would double back to Kaufman County in time for the 9 a.m. court docket. During work, the detail got a break. Occasionally I had lunch plans away from the courthouse, but during those twenty-one days of the detail, usually lunch was brought in. If I was inside the courthouse safe, it gave the guys on the detail an opportunity to check on other work assignments that they had been pulled off of to protect our county during this crisis.

My staff usually informed the detail when I was leaving. Sometimes I had to pick up Jacob after school, but that responsibility was shared and Aaron usually picked up Jacob, and if Aaron couldn't do it, Jacob's older brother, Brad, did.

After work, we had to keep going—both the detail and I. They accompanied me everywhere: to the grocery store, to drop off dry cleaning, to doctor's appointments, to the baseball field at Bishop Lynch.

I spent my days running between dockets and meetings all day. Then I had the kids' extracurricular activities and community and board meetings in the evenings. The task of checking on my elderly father and aunt, who both lived near me, fell to me. I also worked as an adjunct professor at a local university one night of the week.

My detail knew they had a busy target.

As the youngest of the countywide elected officials at that time, and a woman to boot, busy seemed part of my job description. Like my male colleagues, I had a mountain of responsibilities at work. Unlike them, I did not have a wife to handle all the fine details and minutiae of my personal life. In my case, I was the wife. As such, both the mountain and the minutiae were in my purview.

A conversation with my husband brought that home.

After hiding out in my room, away from the security detail, and finishing the unsettling phone conversation with Kim, I lay back on the chaise and dozed off. I awoke to the sound of Aaron's voice and the door to our bedroom opening.

"The guys on the detail said you were back in the bedroom and you hadn't come out for a while after you were on the phone," he said. "I called a few times, you didn't answer, but I wasn't worried. That's the great thing about this detail: if you don't answer, I'm not worried. I know you are covered."

He was grinning.

"Also, would you talk to the kids about keeping a schedule with the detail?" he said.

"Well, it's not funny," I said. "I have to lock myself in my bedroom to have a private conversation. Where were you? I tried calling you before I left today. There is something I want to talk to you about." I was trying my best to answer his questions, but the issue of DA was the topic uppermost on my mind that I wanted to discuss with him.

"They need to know what our schedules are," he continued, ignoring what I said. "They are supposed to know who is coming in and out of the house. That includes the kids."

Then he answered my question.

"I was in court all day today," he said. "I've got duty this week. You know how hectic that can be."

"Duty" at the US Attorney's Office in the Northern District, where Aaron worked, meant that an Assistant United States Attorney (AUSA) took calls, worked citizen walk-ins, and made court appearances for other attorneys, if the assigned attorney had a conflict. It was an additional rotated assignment on top of regular caseloads, but it was a good system—unless you were the one who was on duty.

Without coming right out and saying it, Aaron was saying he didn't want to confront the kids. He did not want any hassles or conflict during this stressful time. Sometimes being the stepdad meant knowing what issues to handle and which ones to pass off to Mom.

Later on in the evening, the kids returned home from school. Brad had picked his brother up from school, and I talked to them both about the importance of a schedule, without incident. The kids knew how deadly serious the situation was, even if we tried to downplay it. They had armed federal agents in their dining room and patrolling our property.

We ate dinner and offered the agents food. But except for a bite of peach cobbler that I insisted on one of them trying, no one ever ate on duty. They were strictly professional.

After dinner, but before bed, we usually watched television in our den, but it was too awkward with all the extra guests looking on. We headed back to our bedroom. Jacob went upstairs to do his homework after dinner. I could hear him overhead, rocking back on the back legs of the chair as he studied. Brad had been at baseball practice and doing "stuff," whatever that entailed for a high school senior. That was his explanation for why he and Jacob were late getting home for dinner. After gulping his dinner, he assured us he had no homework, but that he had to go back to school to emcee a girls' softball game.

In our previous life, I usually heard the door chime when the kids came home, but the agents had turned the chime off at night, so as not to wake us, since they moved in and out of our residence as they took turns on patrol.

The detail worked in three shifts: from 6 a.m. to 2 p.m., 2 p.m. to 10 p.m., and 10 p.m. to 6 a.m. The evening surveillance differed from the day detail, perhaps because danger seems to be harder to elude at night. The agents used different types of weapons, with additional firepower. They took post outside and during the night they walked the perimeter on a schedule. They seemed more serious as a whole on the evening shift. If someone wanted to harm us, night would be an opportune time and the assailant would have the cover of darkness.

This is why they were so very serious about knowing the family's schedules, especially after sunset, when it was dark. They wanted to know what time to expect people coming in and out of the residence.

Brad was usually vague about what time the softball game was ending and what time he would be returning home when I asked him. I told him he had to also inform the agents of his schedule.

But when Dean, the lead agent, asked him about his schedule, he gave his usual nonchalant answer, "I'm in around 10 during the weekdays."

"It's non-negotiable," said Dean. "For everyone's safety, I need to know your plans. This isn't your mom asking." Dean was one of my favorite agents. He was friendly, but professional. He needed to know daily what the planned activities of our household were, when we were coming and going from the house, and what scheduled guests were planned on coming to our home.

I think Dean was also "backing my play" as a parent because Brad had no idea that they had put trackers in all of our cars and knew where we were at all times anyway. After learning about the trackers, Brad clarified his schedule with the agents, in a hurry.

That evening I heard the garage door going up and glanced at my watch. It was 9:55. Brad had made it home, with five minutes to spare. Agents were good for safety, but they also helped with wary teenagers.

IN SPITE OF having to lock myself in the bedroom to talk to my friend, the next day was a little easier than the first couple of days and nights with a security detail.

On the first day, we didn't have federal agents. We had sheriff's deputies. They were parked in the cul-de-sac in a marked car alongside our house. It gave the sheriff's deputies a view of individuals coming into the neighborhood, as well as visibility into our house. Later, I learned from the federal agents a that sitting in a car was not the safest approach to protecting a target, nor was it for the agents who were sitting ducks in the car. So, when the federal agents began their detail, they set up the staging area for their security inside our home in our dining room.

I saw firsthand how the federal security approach worked better. When the deputies were first at our home, it was Easter Sunday. I had to prepare Sunday dinner and I had my family coming to my home. Deputies milled around outside as my family arrived.

Then, something the deputies did not expect happened: FBI agents came to the house to get a search warrant signed. Signing a search warrant is a typical responsibility of a judge. It wasn't out of the ordinary for them to come to my home after hours or on a weekend. The murders had happened in my community of Forney, and at the time the other judges were also out of the county. I don't know if the federal agents knew that the deputies were on our detail that Sunday.

Long story short, we almost had a shootout on the front lawn.

As the federal agents barreled into the neighborhood and parked in the driveway, they either didn't notice the deputies' squad cars or weren't aware the car was there for our protection. They hopped out of their unmarked vehicle, moving quickly to our front door.

The problem was that the deputies initially didn't know who the federal agents were. The agents coming to the door were in plainclothes and simply looked like two men with handguns under their shirts.

By the time I answered my front door, the sheriff's deputy was making his way to the front door, hand on his gun, safety off. In that instant, he must have thought that we might be the next family to be killed by the unknown assailants hunting down prosecutors.

After a few tense moments, everyone calmed down and identified themselves. Meanwhile, my brother was parking his car as this melodrama unfolded in the front yard. He bore witness to it all. I ushered the agents through the front door and into the house to review the affidavit and warrant. The deputies were again at ease; as they took their post back outside. My brother, Homer, who was coming in through the open garage door from the rear of the house, had to retell the near shoot-out during our Easter dinner.

That incident aside, we all settled into our new normal. Our house started to feel like home again, even with a security detail in tow.

The agents used our dining room as the command center and staging area. Because it housed a table and chairs, the guards were able to sit around the table if they weren't outside walking post. The dining room also provided the best view of all the entries into the house.

Most importantly, it gave the detail quick access to my family and me. They had even determined a place we should go in the event of a threat at the house: our safe room.

I no longer jumped or was uneasy in the evening when the surveillance team set up for the late shifts. I no longer resented my armed companions as I walked the dog around at night with someone from the detail—even in my own backyard.

Bottom line? I knew that if anything happened, I was safer with them here than not. It was starting to become more familiar and certainly more comforting.

Chapter 10
Decisions, Decisions

AARON LOOKED AT me as we lay in bed a few days after our detail was assigned. He didn't mute the TV, but turned the volume down very low. We knew that you could not hear through our door once it was shut, but we still wanted to insure our privacy.

"So?" he said, waiting.

I couldn't help myself.

"So, what?"

"You know what I'm talking about," he said. "Are you interested in the position as DA?"

He gazed at me, his eyes steady and serious.

"I don't know," I said. "Are you trying to kill me?"

I was only half-joking.

"Are you serious?" he said. "I love you. I would never do anything to hurt you. You got to believe that."

"I know," I said, softening. This obviously wasn't a time to joke. "It's just crazy—"

"Start from the beginning," he interjected. We hadn't had a chance to discuss me throwing my name in the District Attorney appointment ring.

I explained my conversation with the other judges at our meeting. I circled back through the applicants: the two strong ones that dropped out, and the two good ones that were still in, as well as some of the concerns that the other judges had expressed. I told Aaron that the sheriff came in as the applicants were being discussed, and then Judge Tygrett dropped the bomb—that I should be the next Kaufman County Criminal DA.

"Do you think he would offer you up to be killed, to save his own hide?" Aaron said, fuming.

"Well, politically, aren't you suggesting the same thing?" I countered. "I can tell by your tone that you think it's a good idea."

"No, it's not the same," he said. "I think it would be a good idea because I think you are the most qualified and you have strong ties to this county.

"More than that, these agents will be gone in twenty-one days," he continued. "They will reassess if they are staying, and that's a decision from up the chain of command."

He pointed toward our ceiling and continued.

"When the dust settles and we still can't make a case against the killer, you may still have a detail and security if you are the District Attorney," he said, raising his voice. "The guy wants to kill you. If you are one of one, instead of one of the four judges, your chances are better of not getting killed."

It was the first time my internal light bulb started flickering on. I knew Aaron believed that Williams wanted me dead (and had for a long time). He thought that I would be more protected as the District Attorney.

But now he was fuming, having worked himself up, thinking about the earlier conversations I had had with my judicial colleagues and what their motives may have been.

"Shhh!" I said, whispering. "The agents are going to think we are having an argument."

"No, they know me," he said, flashing his best sly grin. "They'll think I'm screaming for other reasons."

"You've got to be kidding," I said, blushing. "There is a room full of agents walking around in my dining room. I'm not thinking about sex."

I don't know why I blushed. Aaron and I had been married for ten years at that point. It just seemed strange that the agents knew we might be making love. I wondered if Aaron had said something to the guys on the detail.

"You didn't say anything, did you?" I narrowed my eyes.

"Of course not," he said. "I'm a married man. This isn't the locker room. But by the way, they know we have sex."

He gave me a reassuring squeeze and gently began to rub my shoulders. He probably thought the worst part of the detail was having a bunch of guys in the other room while he was trying to be romantic with his wife. Still, it seemed he was willing to give it a try.

"Baby, it's late," he said. "Let's go to sleep. We're not going to solve anything tonight. There are only two things I want you to do."

"Okay, what is that?" I asked.

"Don't say no," he countered.

"What?" I asked, puzzled.

"Don't say no to the idea of being the DA," he continued. "Think about it."

"I will," I said. "I really will. What's the other thing?"

He grinned. He could be charming and that smile—well it was pretty sexy; it always worked on me.

"You know . . ." he said, his voice trailing off.

He turned the volume up on the TV and changed the channel to a music station, sliding his arm around me. I mumbled something, but he ignored me. He wasn't taking "no" for an answer.

I NEEDED TO talk to the sheriff before I made my final decision. From the look on his face the day before, I had a good idea of what his opinion might be.

I didn't have to wait long. By the time I got to my office at 9 a.m. the next morning, he was already there. He had probably been up for hours and left his house by 6. I knew they were having daily briefings at the armory, where military reservists had been trained in bygone days. The armory today was undergoing a renovation to transform into Kaufman County's 911 Emergency Center, and was presently the hub of operations for law enforcement as the investigation of the murders continued.

I still don't know how the sheriff managed those twelve- to fourteen-hour days or longer in his seventies; I was having problems managing it all at forty-nine.

No matter what time of the day or night, he never seemed wrinkled or mussed. His khaki uniform stayed impeccable. It fit him better than it did most of the other, younger deputies. He finished off his sheriff's uniform with black cowboy boots and a white Stetson.

That day, he held his hat in his hands as he waited for me outside my office, in my small waiting room.

"Why am I not surprised that you're here?" I asked, giving him a big smile. Even though he was a serious man, I usually managed to get a smile out of him.

"Can we talk, Judge?" he asked, as he stood up.

He was from a different, more gentlemanly generation. He stepped back as I headed toward my inner office, my judge's chambers.

"Good morning Katie," I said to my coordinator at her traditional station outside my office, not pausing to take a breath. "How 're you? Where's Kim?" There were many attorneys and members of the public that would try to discuss cases with a judge (to get an advantage in a case by providing them evidence outside of the courtroom). Every judge had someone—in my case, Katie—to be a friendly roadblock to the public. With her training and experience, she knew who I could see and who I couldn't see without a pre-screened appointment.

"Fine," she said, matching my rapid-fire tone and grabbing my bags. "Doctor's appointment. I've got those," she said, pointing to my handbag and briefcase. Coffee, Judge? Sheriff? Donut? Someone brought by a box this morning."

"Lovely," I said, smiling. "Aren't you being nice?"

I usually poured my own coffee.

"No, thank you," Sheriff said to her. "I've had plenty."

He had probably had his first cup hours before and was closer to wanting lunch. From experience, I knew he wasn't a snacker, never eating between meals. He ate a solid three meals per day, with not much junk food in between. Desserts for him were few and far between, unless his favorites were on the table: pound cake, cobbler, and cherry pie.

Before Katie turned around to the coffee machine, she threw a friendly jab my way.

"Where are our goons?" she said, grinning.

She kept thinking there would be a cute single one in the group. At twenty-seven years old, she was an attractive woman looking for a fresh start. She had recovered from the childbirth loss of her special-needs daughter, Emma Kate, and the divorce that followed in the wake of the baby's death, and was in need of a fresh start.

I had so much respect for her. I kept telling her the right guy was out there for her. While I did not think that guy was on my detail, I answered her anyway.

"I told Steve—by the way, he is happily married—that I wasn't going anywhere today," I said. "Do you mind ordering lunch in?"

Before she could answer, I rambled on.

"So, I told them I was safe here, and there was no reason to sit in the hallway or clutter up this tiny waiting room," I said. "I told them if I changed my mind I would call them. You have their numbers, right?"

Sheriff cleared his throat.

"Can we talk?" he said, glancing at his watch. It was 9:20 a.m. "I've got to meet someone at 10."

"Sure, sorry," I said.

I had to remember that this wasn't like a week ago, when our only timelines were our own schedules. Now, he was in the middle of an investigation that had grabbed the national spotlight.

I walked into my office and sat behind my desk.

"May I shut the door?" he asked, before taking his usual seat.

"Judge, here is your coffee," Katie said, as she walked in and handed me my steaming cup.

Hearing what sheriff said, she shut the door behind herself. She didn't know about the DA appointment, but we had worked together long enough that she must have suspected that something was afoot.

With the door shut, I started, "I know—"

"You don't know what I'm going to say, so just hear me out," Sheriff Byrnes said, uncharacteristically cutting me short.

He took a deep breath. Sheriff never seemed unsteady or unsure of himself. All of a sudden, he was both.

"You are without a doubt the most qualified person for this job," he said. "You know more than ten years ago, I tried to get you to run for the District Attorney position."

He then smiled for the first time since entering my office that morning.

We had a long history, and I knew he wanted me to run for DA several years ago, but at the time I didn't think I could do it because my children were too young.

Then, his smile faded.

I could read his thoughts. He was not going to be deterred.

"This isn't about qualifications," he said, earnest once more. "This is about your life. There is someone—yes, it's probably Eric, and if you take this job, he will want to kill you. He probably already wants to kill you. Don't wave a red flag in front of him."

He looked at me and I smiled the best charming smile I had, one that always worked. In some ways, he and I were closer philosophically, particularly in regards to our feelings about law enforcement, than I was with my own dad.

"You know I'm going to be okay," I said. "You know that no one is going to kill me, but you also know that this is about even more than just qualifications. I was born and raised in Kaufman county." I ticked off with my fingers. "I'm qualified, I'm from here, and I've already held office, so I know this community," I finished my trifecta.

I knew Sheriff wasn't born in Kaufman County, so I paused before continuing.

"I'm not saying that everyone that is in elected office has to be Kaufman County, born and raised, but we need someone that will make the county feel like they are one of them and restore calm while find the killer," I said. "I'm afraid that some of our citizens may really be fearful. Afraid to go to dinner, to go out shopping . . . it would affect our local economy . . ." my voice trailed off.

"You're right," he said. "This is serious stuff, deadly serious. We have a serial killer on the loose." And then he returned to his original theme, "But it can't be you for DA."

"I've talked to Aaron—" I said.

His look stopped me.

"I'm telling you," he said, clearing his throat. "I don't know if I can protect you from someone that is willing to kill people this boldly. Once in broad open daylight—"

He pointed in the direction of Mark's crime scene toward my window with the closed blinds.

"And the other, a home invasion," he said. "This person has struck three times. And if I can't protect you . . . I couldn't take that, kiddo." His voice trailed off and his eyes moistened as he gazed at me.

I got it. He thought the next DA would be a target. The bulls-eye would be on me if I took the job and he was saying he couldn't guarantee my safety. Who could make that guarantee anyway? He knew if he couldn't protect me, if I got killed . . . Maybe I was insane to consider this job as district attorney.

"I'm not nuts and I don't have a death wish," I said, reassuring both of us. "I think the community needs someone like me and maybe I want to do it."

I paused, thinking that last statement was a bit dramatic or at least egotistical.

"No, you are right," he said. "I've said it before—you are the best person for this job. I've wanted you in the job before."

I heard his sentiments, but his body language belied his words. He was shaking his head from side to side, nonverbally screaming "no!"

"This is real danger, Erleigh," he said, looking me squarely in the eye. "This is life and death and I want you to understand that. You will always have my support, you always have, but it is against my advice if you decide to take this job."

He was deadly serious.

No smile.

No blink.

He was speaking quietly and more deliberately than usual.

"I do understand," I said, reaching over and patting the hand that still held his Stetson. "I appreciate you."

I gave him a lame smile. I could not formulate the words to express how much I appreciated this man in this moment.

He was the most progressive seventy-year-old white man I knew; despite having every stereotypical reason to be a redneck, he wasn't. He was comfortable around people of all colors, he promoted women at the Kaufman County Sheriff's Department, and he abhorred people who mocked or took advantage of those with disabilities.

I knew the advice he gave me was sound. I knew it was from the heart. I had started to tell him Aaron's perspective, and he interrupted me, but now I'm glad he did. I wasn't ready to share Aaron's theory with him yet: that maybe by taking the job, I would be safer.

I knew Sheriff wouldn't appreciate that type of thinking. He was a guy that took things straight on and right now our county had a killer that was shooting county officials and anyone else that got in his way.

Chapter 11
Earl Cabell of Kaufman County?

EVERYTHING THE SHERIFF had said to me came from the heart. I was touched by his sincerity and moved by his concerns. Ironically, not less than an hour later, Judge Tygrett wanted to discuss the District Attorney position with me.

"Judge?" Katie asked, as she placed her phone in the receiver. "That was Kelly."

Kelly Blaine was Judge Tygrett's Court Coordinator, who had the same functions as Katie. She also handled making most of his appointments.

I could hear Katie standing up in her office. Whatever she wanted to say, she didn't want to be overheard by our informal system of yelling back and forth to each other. She popped her head into my chambers.

"Judge Tygrett wants to know if you are available this morning," she said, smiling. "He only needs a few minutes."

We both knew lawyers and judges never talked for a few minutes. Katie was good, I thought again for the hundredth time. We had been together long enough that she knew what to assume and what not to. She wasn't sure if I wanted to get into a long conversation with Judge Tygrett.

I understood why.

My relationship with Judge Tygrett had always been friendly, but guarded. I suspected that he wanted to talk to me about seeking the governor's appointment for district attorney, which was something I hadn't yet shared with my staff. If I became the appointed DA, I unfortunately wouldn't take Katie with me to the DA's office because the office manager/administrative supervisor position was already filled. Firing people and bringing in your own staff under these circumstances would not be a good idea. Ideally, the new judge appointed after I vacated the position as judge would keep Katie on as the court coordinator. It would be the smart move.

I glanced at my watch. It was now 10:45.

"Don't I have a couple of trial announcements set at 11?" I inquired, glancing up at Katie.

"You have exactly two trial announcements," she said. "You had a contested motion to suppress, but they called in and asked to be taken off the docket. They worked out a plea."

She knew cancelled hearings were a pet peeve of mine. Attorneys liked setting hearings, then cancelling them over the phone. Without a court managing the cases, the matters wouldn't get rescheduled and then cases languished without a new setting. This resulted in court delays, clogged dockets, and general inefficiency.

"Judge, they are coming in this afternoon and signing the pass slip," Katie smoothly interjected. "They are set in May on a Thursday court docket. And the defendant will have all his court costs and fine the day of the plea."

She had that smug look. Her expression said, *I got this.*

"Well, tell Judge Tygrett I've got time after the docket," I said. "It should go quick. About 11:30."

"I could always tell him you have a contested motion to sup-press, if you want me to—" Katie said, with a devilish smile.

"I'm fine," I said. "No reason to put him off. I'm sure he has something he wants to tell me."

I pushed back from my desk and headed into the courtroom to finish up my morning court docket.

"**HEAR ME OUT,** Judge," Judge Tygrett began.

He sat in my office, across the desk from me, with his legs stretched out. He clasped his hands around his generous midsection.

I looked up at him. Although he was a few months younger than the sheriff, he could not be more different. Sheriff was slim and walked upright, always seemingly with purpose. Judge Tygrett's hair was totally white and even though he worked on reducing his girth, he was still portly and slow gaited.

I fought the urge to check my phone or glance at the notes on my desk. As he began speaking, I gave him my full attention.

"When President Kennedy was killed . . ." he said.

I'm sure my eyes widened a bit because I had no idea where this conversation was going. President Kennedy was killed in 1963 in Dallas. It was a fateful point in history and the year I was born, but it had nothing to do with the events happening in Kaufman County in 2013.

"Were you born yet?" he said, interrupting himself.

"Yes sir," I said. "I was about six months old."

Because of its historical significance, it was a question Baby Boomers often asked younger people when they recounted where they were when they received the news of President Kennedy's assassination. My friends' answers were much like mine—either we were not born yet or were only months old. We had no memory besides what we had read in our history books and had learned from our elders.

Now that I was more mature, I could relate to my Baby Boomer friends. Generation X had a similar disconnect with the younger generation of Millennials, with more recent events of national significance, like the *Challenger* explosion, the Oklahoma City bombing, and the terrorist attacks of September 11.

Judge Tygrett circled back to his original point, moving his clasped hands from his midsection to behind his head, but keeping my gaze.

"My point"—he paused, his mind traveling more than fifty years back to those fateful events—"is that when President Kennedy was killed—for those of us that remember," he said, "I remember: I was clerking for Judge Estes."

Judge Estes was a US Federal Judge who served in the Northern District of Texas actively from 1955 to 1972. Howard Tygrett had been a law clerk for Judge Estes upon graduation from SMU Law School, an experience he fondly recalled from fifty years before. The Judge had been Howard Tygrett's hero and mentor.

"It was a terrible time for the citizens of the City of Dallas," Judge Tygrett said. "People were stunned. The national attention was overwhelming, but after the media left, we were left with our shame."

He lowered his voice.

It was hard to imagine that almost fifty years later, his voice still shook as he recounted those terrible days. Remarkably, he still felt the pain of a fifty-year-old wound.

"Do you know who Earl Cabell is?" he asked, interrupting my reverie.

"No, I don't," I said.

My mind was beginning to wander and I was starting to get annoyed with the Q&A session, along with the history lesson, that to me was going nowhere. I glanced at my watch. It was 11:45

and my stomach was rumbling. In the midst of my frustration, I realized that Judge Tygrett was waiting for my answer. I focused on his question, and it suddenly came to me. The Earl Cabell building was the name of the federal courthouse where my husband worked.

"The federal building," I mumbled. "It's named the Earl Cabell Federal Building."

"Exactly!" he said, warming to his subject. "Earl Cabell was the mayor of Dallas during the Kennedy assassination. It was dark days for us. It didn't matter if you were Republican or Democrat. The president was assassinated here in our hometown, but Earl Cabell led us through that time as mayor."

Now I understood.

Judge Tygrett was drawing a comparison between what happened in Dallas fifty years ago and the assassinations of Mark, Mike, and Cynthia.

He leaned forward, never dropping his gaze. He was serious.

"We need an Earl Cabell right now in Kaufman County," he said. "You could be that person."

I had never taken Judge Tygrett's urging seriously about seeking the appointment for district attorney. I always thought his motivation was personal, not professional.

After all, he had certainly heard the rumor circulating around the courthouse that I was intending on running against him to be judge of the 86th District Court. In truth, it wasn't a rumor. It was fact. It had been a hard choice. Running against an incumbent and a colleague is never an easy decision, even if I thought I could do a better job.

We also all knew that Judge Tygrett would be seventy-four years old in 2014, turning seventy-five soon after the 2015 term began. The Texas Legislature caps the age for judges at seventy-five years old, unless the judge is already on the bench. In that case, someone of that age or older could finish out an existing term.

In the past, I had known a handful of good judges who'd turned seventy-five in the middle of their elected terms and were ousted before the term was complete. I didn't believe that the intent of the Legislature was to have a judge reach his or her seventy-fifth birthday after they began their terms, but like all good legislation, there were always loopholes.

If I received the District Attorney appointment, I would have to run for reelection in 2014 for that position, not for judge of the 86th District Court. If he had his way, my new best friend and self-proclaimed historian who sat opposite my desk would hold tight to his current position, but I began to wonder—did it really matter anymore? Today we had a new set of facts, and political fortunes were like that. A day could be a lifetime. And the political landscape had changed.

"I didn't know Earl Cabell's story," I said. "I had always assumed he had been some famous federal judge from back in the day."

I stood up to end the meeting. It was almost noon. I extended my hand.

"Thank you for sharing that story, Howard," I said, feeling generous. "I appreciate it and your kind comparison, but I don't think I'm deserving of it. That's quite a compliment."

He returned the smile, again asked me to truly consider the appointment, and then left my chambers.

Certainly I didn't know Judge Tygrett's true motivation, but he was totally sincere in how he felt about the past and the present in Kaufman County. After speaking to him, my notion of his motivations felt petty because I knew that what he had recounted about Earl Cabell was heartfelt. Being compared to a mayor that helped bring Dallas out of the "dark day of shame" was flattering. I had to admit that Judge Tygrett had just done one of his best closing arguments.

Chapter 12
The Devil Is in the Details

OVER THE NEXT few days, I spoke to the other judges individually and expressed my interest in pursuing the position of District Attorney. They were all very encouraging, and generally glad that I was considering the position. The only downside of taking the position, aside from the obvious safety issue, was giving up the bench for a job that was more time-consuming, more work, and more stress.

Because of my decision to consider the DA position, I had excused myself from any further judges' meetings. The judges were going to make recommendations to the governor's office, but ultimately the final choice would be up to the governor. So it was surprising when Katie stuck her head in my office and said that Judge Wood requested a lunch meeting today. She relayed that he was sorry for the short notice, but it was important that I attend the meeting.

She had a slight frown on her face. She and I had planned to do something different for lunch; instead of eating in—my new usual—we were going to go out to lunch. Katie was my constant lunch companion, and lots of times, I would rather have lunch with her and discuss "girl stuff" than have a work-filled lunch with the male Judges, but this meeting sounded different.

"Let him know I'll be there," I said.

"What do you want for lunch?" she asked.

"I don't care," I glanced at my watch. It was only 10:30. "Get whatever you want and make it two. I'm going back in."

I pointed toward the door that led to my courtroom.

"Your recess is over," she said, looking disappointed due to the change of plans.

"Lunch will be my treat," I said.

"You don't have to do that," she said, smiling.

"I want to," I said, handing her a $20 bill. "Is everyone back in the courtroom?"

"Yes ma'am," Katie said.

". . . and that's what the email said," Judge Wood finished. I was puzzled and I'm sure my face reflected it. I looked at the other faces in Judge Wood's office; theirs mirrored my own. The five judges and Sheriff Byrnes were sitting around Judge Wood's conference table. After our minds absorbed the email that Judge Wood read, we finally broke the silence.

"What criminal has ever cared about the judges with such specificity?" someone asked.

Some context: The Kaufman County Crime-Stoppers' Tip Line had received a tip, addressed to Judge Wood.

The tip line was a resource for a witness to communicate anonymous information to law enforcement without the tipster's identity being divulged. If the information proved to be truthful and led to an arrest, the Crime-Stoppers organization would pay the source for the tip. Tip Line information is transmitted by phone and/or Internet.

The tip in question stated, in part, "that one of the four judges needed to resign their position" as "a show of good faith." Within the tip email, the tipster had described details about the murders that had not been publicly released, which made the tip seem credible.

Sheriff Byrnes, who seemed livelier than he had in days, explained the information to the five members of the judiciary. "This is a legitimate break in the case," he said. "This is the first real tip we've had in the case."

Sheriff continued to answer questions from the others, but my mind wandered. In the beginning with Mark's murder, I had not been convinced Eric Williams was the prime suspect. I still had some doubts. It was not until Mike and Cynthia were killed that I begin to accept that he was the only one with a motive for both crime scenes. Aaron had never wavered from Eric as suspect number one, not even with Eric's ready excuse of a shoulder injury when Mark was shot.

Later, during the investigation, as investigators closed in on Williams, it became clear that he liked using the tip line. And for good reason—he wanted to confuse the detectives in the investigation. What better means than an anonymous investigative tool?

Later, as the investigation widened and the police searched his home, the law enforcement who were part of the search found the unique number written on a notepad besides Eric's computer. That unique number was the same number that corresponded to the Crime-Stoppers tip line identifying information. Ironically, he left the trail of the unique number that was designed to protect his real identity.

As I refocused on the questions circling around, I knew that this tip was a break, but only the first one. We finally had more than just our hunches to go on. Ultimately, the facts would lead us to Eric Williams.

Sheriff was explaining why law enforcement felt good about the accuracy of the information in the tip. As stated before, there was information that only the murderer would know. At that point of the investigation, only the police and the killer knew the type of weapon used in the murder of Mark Hasse. From where we had been in the investigation, any news felt like big news.

Eureka! At this point we were getting closer.

Chapter 13
Days of Our Lives

THE DAILY ACTIVITIES of my family's lives consumed Aaron and me and the boys over that next weekend, we had many outings already planned. The only exception to our usual weekend plans was my group of constant companions, formally known as a federal security detail, who literally never left my side.

By then, we had been together for a week so the detail was still professional, but a little friendlier. They had started to learn our schedule, our likes and dislikes. And we began to learn more about them. We knew their names and some personal information such as their wives' names, the number of kids that they had, and some of their hobbies when they weren't at work.

With the weekend baseball tournament, our eldest son Brad's high school baseball games had become quite interesting with the addition of three armed federal agents. They had impressed upon me to not change my schedule, so with me attending the games, the agents were in tow.

Brad attended Bishop Lynch in East Dallas, about twenty minutes away from our house. That year, Brad was a senior and captain of the baseball team, so me missing a game was not an option, despite the circumstances.

While Brad was not the best player on the team, what he lacked in ability, he made up in leadership. His teammates admired him and he handily won the captain position. He led his team in prayer, was a rallying figure, and encouraged them through play.

Attending his games with the detail was attention grabbing, to say the least. Even though the idea was to fade into the background, it never quite worked. It was usually three men wearing Hawaiian shirts to shield the handguns they wore on their sides and baseball caps with visors pulled low to cover their eyes. One of them usually carried a backpack, which contained a submachine gun.

My detail was the worst-kept secret in the community.

Even though the high school was located in Dallas, there were several families from Kaufman County who attended the same school. Everyone in Kaufman County knew about the shootings, the threats to the elected officials, and the ensuing details that had been assigned.

Initially, the baseball families politely ignored the detail. They quickly, however, grew curious; then downright nosy. The baseball moms were overly friendly, offering homemade cookies, fruit, and water, which none of the detail accepted because the men were on the job.

But over time, they did become part of the backdrop. Brad's team had a lot of games, make-up games, and a tournament game during the early days that the detail was assigned to my family. I think the members of the detail enjoyed that part of the job. Though they were ever watchful of something menacing, they still got to enjoy high school baseball in April. There's hardly anything better.

Aside from family activities, my schedule was ramping up with my community commitments as well. I spent the next weekend volunteering at the Dallas Perot Museum. I had been told by my detail to keep to my regular schedule, so I did. I had volunteered to take a shift as timekeeper for a children's skit, which was part of the Children's Cluster program of Jack and Jill Inc. Jack and Jill is a service organization made up of mothers dedicated to helping other children in the community besides their own. Jack and Jill had a strong mission, nurturing the future of African American leaders. So as a member I did my part and participated in the project.

Children's Cluster is one of the biggest events that the mothers organize and volunteer in the Dallas chapter. I am sure I could have easily begged off, but the detail insisted that I keep to my normal schedule and I wanted to participate with my sisters and the children. I thought it might even be fun, or at least normal.

After two hours of monitoring the skits, my shift ended. I decided to walk around, look at the exhibits displayed, and enjoy the new museum in Dallas. It was a modern edifice inside and out, and leaving without at least looking around would have been a missed opportunity. I spied another Jack and Jill sister, Vickie Blanton. We walked together and made small talk, but then she reminded me just how crazy the circumstances were that I had found myself in.

We were having the usual, "How are you, girl?" exchanges and catching each other up about our children. My sons were senior and sophomore in high school, respectively, while her daughter was a junior. Because of the closeness in our children's ages, we shared our similar experiences of teenagers. Vickie had gotten to know Brad even better because she coordinated the educational training for the annual Jack and Jill Beautillion. Beautillion was an event for African American high school senior graduating men.

The Dallas Jack and Jill chapter hosted the presentation of the graduating senior young men into society. No senior could participate in the festivities until they had completed a rigorous training course, which emphasized hotbed issues: consensual sexual issues on college campuses, law enforcement issues, success in college, community service, etiquette, and finding a place in society as productive young African American men. It was no small challenge to complete. Although it was an admittedly arcane notion, its gallantry had survived through the decades.

"Girrrrl . . . them boys," Vickie said, trilling the "r" with a smile. "They can make you blush. What kids know at eighteen these days."

"I know, I know," I said, nodding. "But you keep it real."

"There is no other way to do it," she said. After a pregnant pause, she lowered her voice and continued on.

"So, you know we have all been praying for you," she said. "No one can believe the mess that is going on in Kaufman. Those people are crazy out there, girl. You know I wouldn't be surprised if they still have Klan out in Kaufman County and you know your black butt would be the first to go."

She patted my hand and gently smiled.

Vickie was also an attorney. She worked as in-house corporate counsel for American Airlines at their world headquarters in the Dallas-Fort Worth metroplex. Although she outwardly conveyed ease and openness, she could be tough underneath. You had to be, to be as successful as she had been in corporate America.

I laughed to myself. I realized she had no idea how crazy things really were.

"Okay, what gives?" Vickie said, tapping her toe a bit. "I feel like I'm missing something here."

"I'm sorry," I said, returning the pat on the arm. "I'm not making fun. I appreciate your concern."

I dropped my voice even lower.

"Yes, it is pretty crazy," I said. "You see over there?"

I pointed to where two men were standing, both with loose shirts on. If you paid close attention, you realized they each wore a concealed handgun.

"Yes, there is a cute brother over there with an equally cute white guy," Vickie said. "So?"

"They don't have kids with them and they aren't really looking at exhibits," I said. "They are my security detail. No one is certain what elected official may be next."

I finished, trying to keep my tone as even and undramatic as possible. It did not have the desired effect.

"Oh my God!" Vickie exclaimed. "I knew you were in danger! Those crazy folks in Kaufman—"

"No, no," I said, interrupting her. "Shhhh! It's not just me. Listen to what I said: all the countywide elected officials and some other people have details and guards. The Feds are helping me out and my family. They are some great people. I've started to get used to them. I feel safer."

I finished, looking down. Now I just felt awkward and embarrassed.

"I probably shouldn't have mentioned it," I said.

"Listen, I'm the one that feels like a fool," Vickie said, reading my thoughts. "I'm rambling on about work and the kids and just barely mentioning you and Kaufman and here you are just taking it all in. Girl, I'm proud of you."

"Thank you," I said, my eyes welling up. "But there is no reason to be proud. I just don't want people to think I'm an idiot. Some people have actually thought I should resign my position."

I thought about Kim, who thought I shouldn't consider an appointment, and my own conflicting thoughts about resigning. I knew that there would be more questions to come if the governor appointed me as Kaufman County District Attorney.

But as of then, only a few people even knew that there was a possibility of me becoming the new District Attorney in Kaufman County, and I wasn't offering that information to anyone else just then.

"I'm proud of you, girl," Vickie repeated. This time, she gave me a hug. Even though she was proud, I was feeling overwhelmed. My thoughts were of my conflicting feelings.

"I wouldn't mind those guys for bodyguards," she said, teasingly changing the subject.

We walked through the second floor of the Perot, admiring the crystals, making idle chitchat, oohing and aahing over the largest piece of amethyst geode either of us had ever seen.

My two bodyguards remained close by, ever present. I realized that I had grown accustomed to them and I felt safe.

Chapter 14
Head of State

FOLLOWING A FAMILY weekend that was filled with outings—baseball, volunteer work, and dining out—the work week still rolled around and I had to get back to work. A phone call the following week from Lance Gooden, our State's Representative, who represents our county at the Texas House of Representatives, called to encourage me. Lance, a young statesman and consummate politician, was also interested in me putting my name in for the appointment for the DA position with the governor's office. He thought it would be good for Kaufman County. I appreciated his support.

Elected at age twenty-eight, Lance was a young prodigy in the field of Texas politics. As he aged, his heart was catching up with his political head. That said, no one could outmaneuver him on making the right political moves for his constituents; as a sophomore legislator, he was already on important committees in Austin. He had served on three committees: Appropriations, County Affairs, and House Administration.

He was still explaining. "Well, I want you to meet the governor and be at the press conference—" he said.

"I don't know what you are talking about," I said, interrupting.

The governor is coming to Kaufman County," he said. "This is huge!"

He was going full-steam ahead at this point, barely pausing for breath.

"You're right," I said. "I didn't know."

"Well, now you do know," he said. "Have you got the appointment app done?" He was referring to the application for the appointment of DA.

"I'm doing it."

"You need to get it done."

"Okay, quit badgering me," I replied, annoyed.

"You do want this?" Lance asked, imploring softly.

At least some humanity had crept into his voice.

"Yes, I do," I said, confidently.

I said it, and I felt it. I had weighed the decision over and over again, and knew that I was the right person for the job. Now I just hoped the governor would think so too. It didn't matter what Judge Tygrett's motives may have been—from the moment he suggested it, the seed had begun to take hold.

I had been an Assistant District Attorney in Dallas County ten years prior, and I would be a DA again, this time in Kaufman County.

This time, I would be the DA—if I received the appointment.

"Well, you need to meet the governor," Lance said. "Are you coming to the press conference?" He was back at the beginning of our conversation.

"No," I said.

"No?" he questioned. "Why?"

"Brandi Fernandez is the interim DA. It's her moment and I'm not going to be a hanger-on at a press conference."

"What?" he said, sounding puzzled. "You're an elected official."

"I know," I said. "I have a docket at nine. I will do my docket, take care of the cases, and then come upstairs and meet the governor, if he's still there, but I won't be at the press conference."

"Whatever," he said, exasperated. "Fine. Knowing the governor, after the press conference he will probably want to meet with the local elected officials. Will you be there depending on the time?"

"Sure," I said, but reiterated, "I'm an elected official, but I'm not the DA. I won't butt in at her press conference with the governor."

"Okay, I got it," Lance said. "Get the app done. Judge, I'll see you at lunch with the governor."

I heard the grin in his voice.

Brandi Fernandez had stepped up to take the job as the acting District Attorney and for that, the county should be forever grateful. At the time she took the position her own safety was uncertain, and I respected her for ignoring that and for stepping up.

But much as I respected her actions, Brandi was still a hard person to figure out. We had swapped girl talk from time to time, talking about diets, kids, and how our weekends went. We also shared a Lubbock, Texas, connection: I went to undergraduate business school there, while she attended Texas Tech Law School. But over time, whatever goodwill our relationship had, she had distanced herself personally and professionally.

She could go from cordially speaking and making firm eye contact to averting her eyes in the hallway if we passed. Only when she had to come to my court would she be professionally courteous, then immediately leave at the earliest opportunity.

Her behavior puzzled me, but I never bothered to ask her why she acted that way. I was a judge and I certainly didn't want to make her any more uncomfortable around me. And frankly, our personal relationship didn't matter for us to do our jobs well—it was probably best to just be professional.

Even though her actions toward me were inconsistent, I never regretted my confidence in her ability to do the job, an opinion that I shared with Mike. Shortly after taking office in 2011, Mike had come to ask me about his staff and my perspective from the bench. He sat in my office and we discussed the assistant DAs who had appeared before me in my court. Then he asked specifically about Brandi. I told him I thought she was bright, a solid prosecutor, and might have gotten passed over during the former administration.

He replied that Judge Chitty had said similarly good things. He also shared that she had been in contact with him during the campaign and he personally felt good about her, even though several attorneys had advised him to get rid of her because she was not trustworthy.

Further, Mike reported that he had heard rumors that she was a "win at all costs." I told him I had heard snippets about her character, but that I had never experienced any of it firsthand and I did not think it was a mistake to keep her.

As it turned out, Mike not only kept Brandi as an Assistant District Attorney, he later promoted her to be his First Assistant to manage the office. She proved to be more than a competent ADA, but behind the scenes with defense attorneys, she was known to toe the line—was it over the line? I don't know.

Leading up to the appointment, DA staff sent supporting letters on their temporary boss's behalf. There were conflicting rumors circulating around the courthouse about the support she enjoyed among the DA employees.

I didn't know for sure. I had only been inside the DA's office once in my ten years as judge. But the rumors from that office had made it downstairs to the first floor of my office. A rumor started that Brandi requested her staff of attorneys to write letters on her behalf to the governor's office and that they were frightened of retaliation if they didn't comply, but who knew if any of those rumors were true; I certainly didn't. It was just as likely that she wouldn't have wanted them to send letters. The position she accepted as interim District Attorney was persuasive in and of itself. I chalked it up to pure courthouse gossip, which always seems to run rampant in times of uncertainty.

THE MORNING OF the governor's press conference in Kaufman County, my security detail had a hard time finding a parking place or a place to drop me off safely in front of the courthouse. The courthouse was packed with cars and the media trucks were everywhere.

My thoughts raced back to the last time the courthouse square looked like this. Thank God it was the just the governor in town this time. The last time it looked like this around the courthouse, Mike and Cynthia had been murdered.

The security detail had no choice but to double-park. They got me out of the car and escorted me to my office. I assured them I would be here all day and had no lunch plans outside the office.

I knew Katie wasn't going to be happy about me ditching her for lunch again. I had forgotten to tell her that the elected officials were having lunch with Governor Perry, but I reasoned his schedule was really tight. I doubted if he would actually have time for a real lunch.

Lance would certainly be ticked off if Governor Perry didn't have time to meet with the elected officials after the press conference. I realized I might be disappointed too. Meeting the governor was no small deal. I smiled, thinking about how upset Lance would be if his plans didn't go perfectly.

"Sorry I'm running late," I said, breezing into my office. "Everyone ready in the courtroom?"

"Yes, everybody—including a lot of the defendants who are upstairs in the hallway—is waiting on the governor," Katie replied. "Is it okay if I go up to the press conference?"

"Absolutely," I said. "Get the bailiff, Richard, in here. Or is he helping with security?"

"No they have enough detail guys," Katie said, slyly smiling. "Good-looking, dark suits, yummy."

I love that girl.

"Okay, you definitely go up," I said. "You can fill me in on the press conference later. I'm doing the docket."

I paused and thought for a minute.

"On second thought, I will go on in," I said, zipping up my voluminous black robe. "I don't need Richard. I'll talk to him in court and send him upstairs to get the defendants."

I smiled as I walked through my door leading to the courtroom. I heard Richard announce me.

That man has eyes and ears everywhere. He always seemed to know when I was about to walk in and the courtroom was filling up with litigants that were set on my docket. He had already gotten them from upstairs and had them filing into their seats on the courtroom benches.

As I sat in my judge's chair on the bench, I took in my courtroom. I had one of the larger rooms as it was one of the original courtrooms built in the 1950s, not part of an addition or a remodel. At more than fifty years old, it was considered a historical landmark.

Because of its age, it had none of the security that newer courthouses enjoyed. Though I had been told it wasn't secure, I did love the windows facing the street in my office and a window in my courtroom, allowing a glimpse to the outside. From the window, you could also hear the quiet buzz of the area—birds chirping, muted conversations, cars passing.

I went through the relatively small docket: calling cases, resetting some, taking pleas on others. But I could hear the whirl of activity outside. From my courtroom windows, I could tell when the governor arrived, as you could hear the entourage that surrounded him. Even though most of the media were already upstairs, I heard a few questions thrown his way.

I looked at Scott Smith, my court reporter. As usual, he was seated below the Judge's bench, but within eye and earshot of the activity of the courtroom, the witness stand, and the Judge.

"Go on up," I said. "We're done here."

I knew everyone wanted to hear the press conference. Who wouldn't? This was big news for Kaufman. The governor of Texas, Rick Perry, was upstairs in the 86th District Courtroom. He was here to comfort the local townspeople. It meant that the state had rallied around us.

It was powerful.

I finished up what I was doing. I took the last court file and stacked it in a metal bucket, alongside the other files that my staff would pick up later. There was no one left in my courtroom and I realized I wanted to see the show firsthand too. My plan was to sneak into the back of the 86th Courtroom to catch a glimpse of the end of the press conference.

I walked upstairs. The back entry to the hallway of the court was blocked off, where court staff entered. Security was really tight.

I walked around to the front courtroom door entrance, where the public accessed the court. It was packed. People were lined up outside the courtroom doors, which were open due to the overflow from the inside, all the way up to the front of the courtroom where the governor was standing.

As I approached, I could hear the questions and answers. Governor Perry was assuring the reporters and citizens that Kaufman County had the full support of the state in the wake of this horrible tragedy.

As I stood at the back of the throng, I got a few crooked fingers encouraging me to move forward and stand in the courtroom to listen. By the time I eased around a few people and into the courtroom, the governor was flanked by the other local judges, the sheriff, Lance, our state's representative, our state senator, Brandi Fernandez, a few other local dignitaries, and his own detail. There were cameras, lights, and microphones everywhere.

"The State of Texas will support this community," Governor Perry said. "We will lend whatever resources we have at our disposal to assist Kaufman County in this time of tragedy."

Governor Perry had the ability to make it seem like he personally knew each and every one of those within the sound of his voice. It was reassuring. If the governor's detail got Katie warm and fuzzy, the governor still had the ability to do the same to me. It felt reassuring to know that he was in charge.

I WAS WALKING back downstairs to my office after the press conference ended. Before I got there, however, the other Judges, the sheriff, the state's representative, and state senator waved me over. There was lunch with Governor Perry in the law library with some of the county and state officials. Lance gave me a hard look that said it all: Stop the false modesty and get your butt upstairs.

I scurried back up the stairs. Governor Perry's security detail stopped me until I was waved in by the other elected officials in the law library.

"She's fine," Governor Perry said.

Someone must have told him who I was.

"She's one of the judges," he explained to them further, turning his eyes on me briefly and then continuing to work the rest of the room. I glanced around the room and saw it was filled with other officials, some members of staff, and security detail. Along one wall of books a makeshift lunch line had formed. Heading over, I told the server, "I'll have the turkey, thank you," I said. Smiling, I took a sandwich box and looked around. Seeing a familiar face, I leaned up to Judge Chitty and whispered in his ear.

"Judge, this is pretty impressive," I said. "Whoever gets this close to the governor?"

Judge Chitty smiled back, his blue eyes twinkling.

"And not pay for it," he added, smiling.

We both chuckled.

Governor Perry had been the governor of Texas for the last fourteen years. He had filled the unexpired term of former President, and then Governor George W. Bush, who vacated the office when he won the White House. Perry then won three consecutive elections. I could barely remember a time when he wasn't the governor.

Over that fourteen-year span, the governor had become a strict conservative. Few people remembered that when Perry started his political career in 1984, he was a Democrat. Over the last thirty years, he had become one of the most powerful Republican officials in the country. Governor Perry had made more appointments throughout the state than any other Texas governor in modern Texas history. He wielded his political power effortlessly. For me, getting this close to a man of Governor Perry's stature would have only happened at a political fundraising event; that would have been too pricey for my judge's salary.

Fundraisers and politics were not in play today and it certainly didn't seem that way for anyone observing the governor. He was the most engaged and sincere person in the room. Even though I smiled back at Judge Chitty, knowing what he meant, I watched the governor mingle and schmooze with admiration. He was definitely at home in our small county law library. Some of the press had been allowed in and was finishing up some of their questions when he turned back toward us.

"Anywhere we can sit down and eat this lunch?" he asked.

We had been awkwardly holding our lunch boxes. No one was certain if we were supposed to sit down and start eating at the big conference table in the law library. No one seemed to want to start until the governor started eating.

As if on cue, his detail opened the door of the law library to a hallway which leads to a jury room, down the hall from the law library.

"Sir, there is a conference room in this area," one of the men from the detail said. No one bothered to correct him that it was a jury room, not a conference room.

"Thank you," Governor Perry said, walking out of the library and into the hallway.

We followed behind him with our lunch boxes.

We sat around a table in the jury room, which was small and cramped. That was one problem with working in a courthouse that had been designated as a historical building: it was hard to alter, even if necessary due to the county's growth.

The group sitting with the governor was some of the same group that had sat around Judge Wood's conference table that fateful Monday, the weekend after the McLellands were killed.

Was that just a week ago? It seemed like a lifetime. So much had happened in such a short time. Our lives had been forever changed.

Governor Perry began speaking.

"A dirt farmer . . . do you know what a dirt farmer is?" he asked, looking at me.

I was sitting to his immediate left. He sat at the head of the table, like a patriarch at a family gathering. The other judges were scattered around the table, as well as the sheriff and state officials.

Lance and I were the youngest at the table: he, by more than twenty years, at only thirty years old; me, by more than ten, at fifty. Everyone else was sixty or over, including the governor. He just didn't look like it. And of course, I was the only woman at the table.

There was no doubt who was in charge in the room.

Governor Perry had opened his lunchbox. It was more of a signal that we could eat because he didn't seem to want to eat. He wanted to talk, and right then, his focus was placed squarely on me.

And I was going to place the sandwich in my mouth. Glad I waited.

"Well, sir, not really sure," I said, smiling. "Sounds like some type of farming practice."

That was lame, but a lawyer could always come up with some type of answer out of the context of the question.

"Dirt farming is farming with no irrigation," he said, smiling patiently. "It's hard. It's brutal and it will make you want to do something else. It did me. I was born in West Texas, in Paint Creek. My dad was a dirt farmer and after I finished college—"

He stopped, seeming to lose his train of thought.

"Any Aggies?" he asked.

We all shook our heads no. I had gone to Texas Tech and Texas Law. The other lawyers were Southern Methodist University graduates. The state officeholders didn't respond; I think they had heard this before.

He kept going, as if he hadn't interrupted himself.

"I went back home to work the family farm," he said. "That's hard work. It makes you start figuring out a few things."

As he spoke, I conjured up an image of young Governor Perry with a hoe in the middle of a vast field.

This is what made this man tough.

I knew this was a story he must have told often because it was what shaped him. Even though there was just a little bit more than a decade between us, he and I were from different generations in Texas. His had been a much harder life in some ways.

As he spoke about dirt farming, and his early years on the farm, we all respectfully listened, but my mind turned to the even harder stories of my mother's youth. My mother was born in 1929. She was raised in a large, poor black family that was rich in love and not much else. Her father had farmed much the same way, even though I had never thought about the term dirt farming until today. My granddad was a sharecropper, where Perry's father owned his land. My mother told stories about picking cotton, walking miles to school, and the segregated

South. Those stories stuck with me. They formed her character and influenced mine.

I shook off those distant memories.

The governor is sitting six inches away from me. I need to be in the moment.

As his farming story started to wane, the other men in the room made polite conversation about farming and how times had changed to commercial farming.

I've got to save this conversation: "So, is that where you met the First Lady of Texas?" I asked.

I had remembered that he and Anita Perry were high school sweethearts. I think the governor appreciated the conversation shift, because he smiled at me.

"Yes, I have known Anita since we were in grade school," he said.

He then began another familiar story for him. I could tell he loved his wife. I liked that about a man. I liked that about my husband. I smiled, thinking about Aaron. I'm sure the governor thought it was for him, since he smiled back.

We then began to talk family—kids, grandkids, the colleges that they attended. I had a graduating high school senior that year who would love to go to Vanderbilt University. He had a son who had already gone there and graduated.

The atmosphere was no doubt collegial. We weren't uncomfortable anymore and began to swap some college stories of our own college days. He even laughed at a familiar Aggie joke. You would have thought the governor had all day and that he sat in the Kaufman County jury room all the time.

Styrofoam was rattling, a clear sign that lunch was finishing up. I glanced at my watch; we had had about fifteen minutes uninterrupted with the governor.

There was a knock on the door. It was one of his aides with a security detail standing behind him.

"Five minutes, Governor," he said respectfully, but firmly.

Rick Perry may have changed his gubernatorial calendar to fit Kaufman County into it, but he was still the governor of a very big and busy state.

Before the door shut, the others in attendance had gotten up and were heading toward the door, following Lance's lead. The men were walking to the head of the table, where the governor had been seated, expressing their thanks and shaking hands with each other.

The governor was standing. I was, too. I thought it was time to leave. The governor turned toward me, presumably to shake my hand. Instead, he had a question for me.

"Do you know Wallace Jefferson?" he asked.

Well, sure. He is the flipping Chief Justice of the Supreme Court of the State of Texas . . . first black guy to have the job, I thought.

"Yes, sir," I said, out loud. "I know Chief Justice Jefferson."

Then the governor sat, so I sat again, too. There was no one left in the room, as the other officials filed out.

"I went to law school with Wallace Jefferson," I said. "I mean, Chief Jefferson. He was a much better student than I was."

I smiled.

The governor wasn't smiling and seemed to be weighing his words. He finally spoke.

"It's hard being a conservative African American," he said. "I admire Chief Jefferson so much."

He looked at me, as if to include me in that admiration, but he was playing it honest. He didn't know me, so he didn't want to be condescending and verbally include me too, just because I was a black Republican as well. But he did know Chief Jefferson and his family's story.

"Jefferson's ancestors were slaves that was brought to Texas through Beaumont," The governor said. "And now, his great-great-grandson is the Chief Justice of the State of Texas."

The governor smiled with pride at his colleague.

"I don't know why no one understands what a compelling story that is," he said, musingly. "It's tough, isn't it?"

He was now looking at me, talking to me, about me.

In that moment, I knew why this man was Governor of one of the most powerful states in our country.

His last presidential run did not convey it through the medium of television, but he had it, that inexplicable, mystical thing that draws people in: charisma.

"Yes, sir," I said, then paused.

He was the governor. I didn't want to rush in, if he was going to continue to talk, but he didn't. He was listening.

"It's tough," I said. "I'm a conservative because it makes sense to me. I don't believe that just giving people the things they want will ever work. I mean, people need to earn the things they need and want."

We both knew there were exceptions: the poor and disadvantaged, the elderly, the mentally and physically disabled. But we didn't have to express it. This was not a "gotcha moment" with media types trying to twist our words. This was a moment shared by two people with shared philosophies.

"It's hard at family gatherings," I said. "Most of my family don't feel that way, or many of my friends for that matter. But my husband does. We truly believe that the government needs to create the right environment for business and growth, but after that, really get out of the way."

I was starting to warm to my topic, but I was a novice talking to a seasoned politico. So I finished quickly.

"But Governor, I'm sure these are things you already know and feel and can express better than me," I said.

"I do, but—" He paused, changing topics midstream. "How old are you, if you don't mind me asking?"

"I'm forty-nine," I said. "I will be fifty in a little over a week."

He smiled genuinely.

"Forty-nine," he said. "You are a baby."

He looked me squarely in the eyes.

"I'm more than ten years older than you," he said. "It was a different time when I grew up. Texas was segregated when I went to school, but not for you, and not for the younger ones coming behind you."

He stood up. I did too. I knew the moment had passed.

He extended his hand. I took it.

"Judge, I appreciate your service to this state," he said. "We are fortunate to have you."

I was humbled. It was political rhetoric, but with my hand in his, it didn't feel like it.

The governor was thinking something. He hesitated only briefly.

"I know these are serious times," he said. "This community has lost three of its own. This is a striking blow to law enforcement. Whatever decisions are made later, know that I will do everything in my power to protect this community." He hesitated and then finished, ". . . and to protect you. To keep you safe."

He finished with a brotherly pat on my shoulders and opened the door. It was the briefest of conservations, it couldn't have been three minutes, but he had an uncanny ability of connecting with people, even in a short period of time.

His aide was right there. With the governor back in hand, the aide started to brief him on the next event. They jostled him away from the law library and down the stairs, where his convoy of SUVs waited.

And then, he was gone. I've never seen him again.

Mike Snipes, Criminal District Judge appointed to preside over the Williams cases.

Eric Williams.
Courtesy of the
Kaufman Herald.

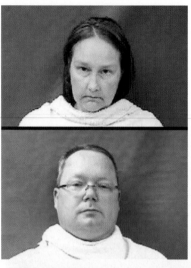

Book-in photos of Kim and Eric Williams. *Courtesy of the Kaufman County Sherriff's Office.*

A cache of guns and evidence secreted by Williams. It was found in Lake Tawakoni by law enforcement divers.

Mark Hasse, Chief Felony Prosecutor, Kaufman County, Texas. *Courtesy of the Hasse family.*

Mike McLelland, Criminal District Attorney, Kaufman County, Texas. *Courtesy of McLelland family.*

Cynthia McLelland. *Courtesy of her daughter, Christina Foreman.*

Erleigh Wiley and her husband, Aaron.

The author's son, Brad, on top of a Homeland Security vehicle.

Chapter 15
Deep in the Heart of Texas

DURING THE APPLICATION process for the appointment of District Attorney, the fact that my name was being submitted as a potential nominee had not been publicly discussed. That wasn't deliberate; after Judge Tygrett asked me, I simply never discussed it with anyone at the courthouse, except him and Sheriff Brynes. Because I never asked anyone at the courthouse for a recommendation to the governor's appointment office, no one knew. I don't think anyone anticipated that I would have an interest. Frankly, the idea had not originally occurred to me.

The essential parties knew: my family, the other judges, David Brynes, and of course the governor's appointment secretary, Darrell Davila. But there was no real reason for me to make it public.

After I submitted the application, the other candidates and I had to travel south to Austin to meet with Governor Perry's appointment secretary and staff. Austin is the state capitol of Texas and lies about two hundred miles from Kaufman, south on Interstate 35.

My plan had been to fly down for the day, hoping to limit this to a one-day trip. After hearing my plans, Lance offered for me to swing by his place to freshen up. If I had time, I would have breakfast, do the interview, then fly back to Dallas in time to pick Jacob up from baseball practice.

Accordingly, my security arrangement had to be adjusted. Because of my flight plans, their schedules would have overlapped, creating logistical issues. Further, clearing their weapons through a commercial airport could be tricky.

I could tell that the unexpected trip and the prospect of me being out of their sight bothered my detail. They were controlling, and took their assignment seriously, and thus didn't like changes in scheduling.

So my one-day business travel came to resemble a set of helicopter parents taking their young child to the airport. One agent checked in with airport security at the curbside. Both men flashed their badges. The car double-parked with impunity. One agent remained with the car; the other agent walked me into the airport and deposited me at security. Because he had his firearm, he had to leave me at the security area. He instructed me to call him when I got on the plane, before the flight crew asked the passengers to turn their phones off. (I later learned that even though I called him as instructed on the plane, he would not leave the airport until he saw that my plane had safely cleared takeoff.) At the other end in Austin, a Texas Department of Public Safety officer met me as I exited the aircraft.

The flight from Dallas to Austin was only an hour from start to finish. At the Austin airport, the sign the officer meeting me held had my name printed in all caps: ERLEIGH WILEY. But I didn't need the sign to recognize that he was there for me—I would have known him anywhere. He had a short-cropped haircut, and was standing tall and soldier-like in a single-breasted dark suit.

He looked nothing like the other car service drivers; his appearance made him stand apart from the others. The Texas Department of Public Service (DPS) is responsible for statewide law enforcement and vehicle regulation. DPS is made up of thirteen divisions, most notably their Texas Highway Patrol State Troopers. Not uniformed, I learned later that my driver was part of another division, the criminal investigative unit, and also worked security detail for statewide elected officials.

"I'm Erleigh Wiley," I said, extending my hand.

I had my purse and a small shoulder carry-on bag with my personal items in it. My interview wasn't until 11:30 a.m., so since my flight was on time, I would have time to freshen up and breakfast.

"It's a pleasure," he said. "Can I take that for you?"

He pointed to my bag. I gladly handed it over. It had started to get heavy. I thought I had probably overdone it in packing the bag, but I had to smile inwardly. A girl has to look good at these things.

He thought my smile was for handling the small, but heavy bag. It was, in part; I also did appreciate him being a gentleman.

"Car's on the curb," he said, smiling good-naturedly. "I've got my ID on the dash, but we don't need to press our luck."

Post 9/11, unattended cars, even those with DPS credentials in the dash, were subject to getting towed. We walked away together toward the exit. An understated dark Ford sedan was parked alongside the curb. He opened the door to the backseat on the passenger side and waited while I slid in. He glanced around as he came around to the driver's side. I wondered if he was even conscious that he was looking around or if it was second nature to look for something out of the ordinary.

What was he looking for, exactly? I wondered.

"Where to?" he asked, sliding in.

It wasn't even 9:30 yet. I knew that Lance had wanted to grab breakfast with me.

"I'm not sure, but I am early. My state rep may want to have breakfast with before the interview at 11:30. Let me check," I said, as I fished for my phone in my handbag.

"That's fine," he said. "I will take you wherever you need. Flight leaves at 14:25."

I had forgotten how efficient these guys were: obviously my Dallas detail had given him my flight arrangements. He probably knew I was trying to get back in time to pick up Jacob, too.

"Got it," I said, as I found my phone.

Turning on the phone, I saw that Lance had already texted me while I was on the plane.

Let's do breakfast, the text read. It included his address.

I texted him back that I was on the way.

"Let's head toward downtown Austin," I told the trooper. "Here's the address."

Lance had a place to stay near the capitol when he was in town on legislative business and not at home in our district.

"No worries," the driver said, pulling the car away from the curb and turning toward downtown.

We ran into morning commuter traffic in Austin, but then again, there always seems to be traffic in Austin these days. Thankfully, my driver navigated his car expertly through it, seeming to know which lane to be in to avoid lengthy stops, and would deftly move to another lane where the traffic was moving. We headed south on I-35 and took the up-ramp, which bypassed many of the exits. We were now picking up speed. Familiar sights flashed by outside my car window: the stadium, the Tower, and the Erwin Center.

We had already passed the law school, where I had spent three years of my life. Sometimes it was hard to remember that girl that had turned twenty-two the month before her arrival in Austin in May 1985. I was a recent college graduate and had gotten accepted into Austin's now defunct summer program.

At that time in my life, the idea of a summer semester appealed to me, having already graduated a semester early from Texas Tech the previous December. I had a silly notion that being a twenty-four-year-old lawyer was a good idea.

In the midst of my recollections, I smiled to myself for the second time that morning. It was at that moment that the trooper looked at me in the rearview. He smiled back.

He thinks I'm an idiot. Every time he looks at me, I'm smiling like a braying mule.

I started to ask him if we were getting close, as he had exited off the interstate, but I couldn't remember his name. I hated that. I'm sure he told me. Before I could ask, we made another turn and there was the capitol. The Texas State Capitol always left me speechless, as it is one of the largest state capitols in the country; in fact, it's larger than the US Capitol in Washington, DC.

He made a few more quick turns and we were pulling up to a glass building. Just then, Lance texted me back.

"He's finishing up. He said he would be ready in a minute." I told the driver, looking up from my phone. "Do you want me to hop up and get him and then we can go?"

I didn't finish my sentence before he politely cut me off.

"No ma'am," he said. "You will not be doing any hopping or getting out of the car without me. We are going to have to park and go up together or—"

He struggled for the name.

"Or Lance . . . I mean Representative Gooden can join us in the vehicle, but I can't stay parked alongside this building very long," he said.

"Sure," I said, mumbling.

Sometimes having security seemed like fun or the ultimate convenience. But in moments like these, it all came crashing back. This was not fun and games, nor was it for my convenience. This was for my protection.

Someone might be trying to kill me.

Even though it was ludicrous to think someone would travel to Austin to kill me when I would be back the same day, the agents that guarded me took the threat seriously. These serious men and women were putting their lives on the line for me. I got that chill again that I sometimes felt when I really thought about the danger.

The phone ringing broke my reverie.

"Where are you?" the familiar voice from the phone inquired.

"Lance, we're downstairs," I said. "Just got here."

Lance had already thought ahead. He asked me to hand my phone to the officer and he gave him directions for parking in the garage and coming on up. After a short visit upstairs, where I got an opportunity to "powder my nose," the three of us ventured out for breakfast.

Our timing was perfect. We found three counter seats at the Counter Café, a little place that the locals liked to frequent. Lance and I ordered, ate, and chatted. The trooper of course did not eat, but drank a glass of water.

Unlike other details, the trooper had to sit with us because of the lack of space in this small restaurant. He didn't join in the conversation and, in fact, tried to act like he didn't hear what we were saying. He just watched everything that was going on around us, while occasionally glancing at a copy of the local newspaper that had been left on the counter stool and generally trying to blend in.

"Judge?" he asked, glancing at his watch and tapping the face of it to remind me of the time.

This made me glance at my own watch. It was 10:45. We paid the bill, got up, and headed toward the car.

We dropped Lance off, with well wishes on my interview. After parking in the garage, I made it into the appointment office by 11:15. The receptionist told Mr. Davila I was there, but she informed me that he wouldn't be available until 11:30.

After I sat down, the officer let me know the rest of the day's itinerary.

"I'm going to stretch my legs, but I will be outside the doorway or waiting for you in here when the interview is over. That should give us plenty of time to make your flight," he said.

"I'm fine," I said. "I'm inside the capitol. There's security here."

"Since we are early, I'd like to go to the restroom," I said, standing up, directing my comment toward the receptionist. She nodded, letting me know she would let Davila know that I was down the hall, if he finished early.

As I headed out the door and toward the direction of the restrooms, I passed the officer, who had taken a seat outside of the appointment office. He politely smiled at me, giving no outward sign that he was my security detail. He blended in with the other people standing and sitting around the capitol, waiting on appointments.

I headed back to the waiting room. In my wait, I had gotten immersed in one of the *Texas Highways* magazines strewn across the waiting room tables and didn't notice that Darrell Davila had entered the room until he was standing in front of where I was seated.

I stood up. He was pleasant and immediately extended his hand.

"Judge Wiley, Darrell Davila," he said. "It is a pleasure."

"Erleigh Wiley," I said. "Mr. Davila, it is my pleasure to meet you, as well."

Davila was an attractive man, and appeared to be in his thirties. He had a strong build and wore his suit well. He appeared completely at ease as I followed him into a small conference room. It was clear he had interviewed many applicants for the various boards, agencies, and offices that the governor was called upon to fill by appointment.

I entered the conference room and sat in the chair across from where Darryl was seated. It was unusual. Having been a judge for ten years, I wasn't generally in the chair across the desk from the person asking the questions.

I found Davila to be direct, engaging, informed, and more than competent at his job. He had interviewed many people who had gone on to high-ranking positions across the state. He and his staff read the applications, did background checks, and vetted the applicants. He made it clear that he did not make the appointment, since the ultimate appointment decision was to be made by Governor Perry.

We went through my resume, experience, and the reasons I wanted the position. It wasn't until we shook hands across the table as I stood to leave that he hesitated. It was clear to me that he was weighing the decision to ask me something.

"Yes, Darrell?" I asked, suddenly now the interviewer. This position felt much more familiar. "Is there something else you wanted to say?"

"I want you to know that you have had many phone calls, letters of support, as well as all the judges supporting you," he said.

"Yes?" I said, my tone urging him to reveal whatever was lurking below the surface of our conversation.

"But . . . there was one negative call," he said. "I'm not at liberty to say, but he—I mean he or she—wanted me to know that while you have been on the bench, you did a favor for an elected official that you liked."

"A favor for someone I work with?" I asked, truly puzzled.

"To put a finer point on the favor, a favor for their son," he said.

Then my mind landed on what he might be talking about, but I couldn't believe it.

"You mean allowing their son to participate in a diversion program. That could hardly be a favor . . . in fact it's more rigorous." The Diversion Court model was an alternative to the traditional court model. The reason it worked so well was because the participants were more closely monitored.

"I'm sure that's what they were talking about," he said. "I remember he mentioned a 'sweetheart deal' on a plea."

He laid a hand on my shoulder, sensing my frustration.

"We all have our detractors," he said. "I'm just letting you know that there was one complaint and the nature of it, but that's all I can say."

As he looked at my face, he knew I wanted to know who called him.

"I'm not at liberty to share the name with you," he said, again.

I knew he was too professional to tell me the name of my complainant, but it didn't matter. I knew the source. But it bothered me that the source never asked me face-to-face about it. He would rather stoop to backhanded smears and try to hurt me in the appointment process.

It also occurred to me that while the courthouse might not have known about my application, they could have; it was a public appointment process and anyone who wanted to know who the applicants were would only have to call and ask.

It's just politics, I thought, inwardly groaning. Part of politics is that you have to accept that you can't please everyone and that doing the right thing is more important than being liked. So having someone that politically disliked me for treating someone fairly shouldn't matter, even if it caused a complaint. I had to remember that my detractor didn't have all the facts and as a judge I couldn't divulge them to him or her.

So I shrugged it off and trudged on, choosing to take the high road.

"No worries," I said out loud. "Thank you again, Darrell. It was a pleasure to meet you."

After the interview, he walked me out of the room and into the waiting room. My trooper was patiently waiting there. He had moved from his outside perch to inside the office waiting area. Away we went.

That day, timing was on my side. I had everything down, all according to schedule.

Back home in Dallas, as I headed south toward Bishop Dunne to pick up Jacob, I closed my eyes and relaxed into the back seat's headrest. While the security detail negotiated through traffic, heading toward the school from the airport, I rested my eyes in the warm sun.

I suddenly realized I never got the DPS trooper's name and I felt bad, but I knew I probably would never see him again. He was a man like so many other men and women who protect us every day but remain nameless.

They may go nameless, but not thankless.

I smiled. That thought made me feel better and for the hundredth time, I thanked God for them. I had never experienced what it was like to be in real danger, like officers do daily, but this experience had showed me what it could be like for my family and me.

I sighed quietly and prayed, "Thank you, Lord, for these men and women. Keep them safe. Keep me and mine safe too."

Chapter 16
I Got the Nod

BY THE SECOND week after the McLellands' murders, my personal life and my work life still had not returned to normal. I realized that a "successful" week now was judged by much different standards than before: success meant no slaughter of additional county officials and progress in the capital murder investigations. For me, there was also the anticipation of the governor's decision about the appointment of the new Kaufman County District Attorney. For a position that I had not originally wanted, I truly wanted the appointment.

My strongest competition for the appointment? Brandi Fernandez.

She had the experience. As stated before, prior to the murders, she had served as Mike McLelland's first assistant. Before that, she had worked for McLelland's predecessor, Rick Harrison.

When McLelland had assumed the position of District Attorney in 2011, there had been questions about Fernandez staying on at the DA's office. But McLelland wanted to be fair and he wanted to make his own decision. To accomplish that, he consulted the judges individually. When asked, I gave him my opinion. I was honest about my limited interaction with Brandi as a judge, but told Mike that the few times she did appear in front of me, she was prepared and more than competent. Further, Fernandez had unhesitatingly accepted the job when Judge Wood appointed her after Mike's murder. Still, Judge Wood's appointment was temporary, lasting only twenty-one days, and a full appointment would have to come from the governor's office.

But now she was seeking the full appointment. The rumor mill in the courthouse was running rampant, with scuttlebutt about the letters of recommendation and the defense attorneys complaining about working with her. There also seemed to be a widespread concern that she wasn't a Kaufman County native, having had moved to Kaufman less than ten years ago for a job. In Kaufman County, ten years still made you a new resident. None of that weighed in her favor.

I had never publicly announced that I was seeking the position as District Attorney. Throwing my name into the rumor mill now would only keep the courthouse frenzy going strong. As the governor was considering the appointment, the uncertainty of his decision was unnerving. I began questioning my decision to seek the appointment. My plate was already full with my family and my job. The thought of becoming a hunted Kaufman County official seemed daunting.

And then I got a call from my brother, Autry, which helped me remember why I had thought about the appointment.

"Sis, how are you doing?" Autry asked.

Autry was the oldest child of our sibling group of five. He was the consummate older brother, a born leader. I was the fourth child and the only girl.

"I'm fine," I responded, with a little sigh.

"You don't sound fine," he said. "What's going on down there? You know I'm always prepared to come home." He lived in Minnesota and was a successful salesman for an international cement supplier.

"No need to come home," I said, trying to sound convincing. "We're all fine."

He had offered many times over the last couple of weeks to "come home" in the face of an emergency. Translation: to sit on the front porch with his shotgun, prepared to kill any would-be assassins. Some people might think that was just bravado, an older brother talking tough. I knew my brother meant it.

He was tough, pure and simple. He always had been.

He had graduated from high school early, at sixteen. A scrawny defensive player, he had made a name for himself in small college football in the early '70s. He was an All-American for four years at the then East Texas State University (now Texas A&M University-Commerce). He went on to play professional football after getting drafted by the Vikings in 1975.

"You've said 'fine' twice, so I'm going to assume you are fine," Autry said. "But I think that you are not okay about something. So I woke up this morning and I knew I had to call and tell you something. Aunt Fern—"

He stopped, his voice getting lost in his throat. The mention of my mother's name still choked him up. She had been gone for almost twenty years. Even though she and my dad raised him and his brother from babies, they always referred to my parents as Aunt Fern and Uncle Homer. When my mother died, we all took it hard but Autry seemed to take it the hardest.

Growing up, Mom had an ability to make everyone feel special and Autry was her golden boy. It never mattered what mistakes he made. She encouraged him to do better and he would do better because he never wanted to disappoint her.

"Aunt Fern was tough and she was always for doing the right thing," he said. "You know when you called me and talked to me about what you were thinking about doing . . . this appointment?" I held my breath, as he searched for his words. I thought he was going to blast my decision like he did when I initially called him.

"Well, I was wrong," he continued. "You are Aunt Fern's daughter. You are tough and you know what is right. This is right. I feel that now. If she were here, she would tell you to do it. If the governor offers you the appointment, you need to accept it."

"Well, it's funny that you are calling," I said. "I was just beginning to wonder if I am nuts for even thinking about this. Maybe I'm going from the fat to the frying pan."

Autry chuckled.

"Nah, Sis," he said. "You're pretty much 'in the grease' wherever you go."

We both chuckled. Suddenly, everything felt better.

We talked about a few more things. Family, work and vacation plans, when he would be home again. We hung up, with a parting "good luck" from my brother. Everything was really fine again.

ON WEDNESDAY, APRIL 10, 2013, I walked into my office a little later and more ruffled than usual. I had had to run an errand after dropping Jacob off ; I had forgotten a fruit tray that I had to bring to the school for the teacher's appreciation party. So I had to double-back and deliver it to the teacher's lounge at the school, after making a quick dash to the local grocery store. One agent waited in the car and one accompanied me inside; the second car had already headed to the courthouse. They were good-natured about it, but I knew they didn't like making unplanned stops.

"Sorry I'm late," I said to Katie, glancing at my watch.

"Anything happening?" I asked. "Anybody ready in the courtroom yet?" It was almost 9:30.

I stopped for a breath as I breezed through the outer offices into my chambers.

Katie looked up. She had a yellow sticky note in her hand, as I stuck my head back around the corner of my door, craning my neck to look at her.

"The attorneys have checked in, but went to other courts," she said. "I told them that you would start the motion hearing at ten and told them to be back, but this seems like it may be more important. He just called and asked me to have you call him as soon as possible."

She handed me the note. I looked at the name: it read Darrell Davila, with area code 512, the area code for the city of Austin.

My stomach did a little flip. Was he calling to tell me that I had it or to politely tell me the governor had gone another way?

I looked at Katie. Her face was expectant.

"Let me call him and then I will fill you in," I told her.

Through the years, regarding work and our personal lives, Katie and I had kept few secrets between us, but I had kept her out of this decision. I knew she would support me in whatever I wanted to do, but she was going to be hesitant about losing me as a boss.

I shut my office door for privacy and dialed the number.

"Darrell," I said evenly. "Erleigh Wiley. How are you?"

"Fine, Judge," he said. "How are you?"

We exchanged pleasantries and then he cut to the chase.

"Judge Wiley, the governor would like to appoint you as the Criminal District Attorney of Kaufman County," he said.

My mind went blank, and the call went silent. I heard the words but I was still surprised. I'd had a good interview, I knew my colleagues supported me, but nothing was ever a done deal.

"Judge, the governor needs to know if you will accept," Davila said, interrupting my mute reverie. "This appointment has to go to the Senate for confirmation. We have a small window, as you know the interim appointment expires soon." He was referring to the twenty-one days.

I took a breath.

"Yes, I will accept the appointment," I said.

Then I remembered my manners. "Please convey to the governor how much I appreciate his confidence in me in making the appointment and my sincere thanks." I added, "And thank you, Darrell."

"Judge, I will let the governor know," he said. "I know he has confidence in you. Have a great day. I've got some more calls to make."

MY HEART WAS pounding, but I had to turn my thoughts to the courthouse, and the hardest part would be talking to Katie. As the Criminal District Attorney, I could ask Katie to become my administrative assistant, but I thought with all the turmoil that had occurred in the DA's office, changing anything wouldn't be fair to the staff. Every employee in the DA's office had earned the right to stay. Also, Katie would be an asset to whoever became the new judge; they would be foolish to not keep her on as their court coordinator.

When I talked to Katie, she reacted exactly as I expected: excited for me personally, but sad for the loss of our working relationship. We had on occasion talked hypothetically about if I left my position as judge, either by running for another position or going into private practice, but it was different now that the once nebulous notion of "leaving" had a looming, very real deadline.

The rest of the morning was typical. I finished the hearing in court, but I knew I needed to call Aaron to share my good news, before the story was released and he heard about it on the news.

"Aaron, this is Erleigh," I said to my husband of nearly a decade.

"I know who this is," Aaron said, chuckling. "What's up?"

"I heard from Darrell Davila," I said, hesitating a bit. "I got it. I'm the new DA." I could hear the smile in his voice.

"I'm proud of you and the county is lucky to have you," he said.

"You are such a homer for me," I said, meaning that I was his favorite home team and he pulled for me at every turn.

"I am," he said. "I'm an Erleigh fan. Make no mistake. It takes nothing away from my masculinity."

He spoke in a funny-sounding voice that he often used to mock himself.

"Whatever," I said, smirking. "I've got stuff to do. I have to get this office ready for the transition for the next judge and start planning for my new job."

New job?! My mind was reeling as the words were being uttered.

"Stop, baby," he said. "Give yourself a minute. Enjoy the moment. It's all going to be there for you. How's Katie?"

"She is the best," I said. "Happy for me, sad for herself. You know she is the number two member of the Erleigh fan club. So she's a little uncertain, but already getting into the transition mode for the next judge. Whoever the new judge is, they will certainly keep her on as their court coordinator. I've assured her anybody would be a fool to get rid of her."

"You are right about Katie," he said. "Have a good day, DA Wiley!"

I could tell he was enjoying my moment and successful appointment. He had thought this was the job for me, even before I did.

As the morning moved into afternoon, the courthouse teemed with the news. There were almost only well wishers, save a disappointed candidate who made her feelings known. Overall, I knew I had made the right decision.

Now, I had to get my court ready for the transition, do the work on the bench, and prepare for a new job. And that was just at work.

At home, things took an unanticipated turn between the detail and me. The agents had always been polite with me, but after the news hit of the governor appointing me to Kaufman's top spot, I think their politeness grew into admiration.

Before the appointment, when we returned home most evenings, Aaron shared camaraderie with the agents that I did not. Even though law enforcement respected judges, we were not part of their team. He and the agents talked about cases that they had together, and they sought his opinion on other criminal matters.

Even though the Kaufman County Criminal District Attorney was not a federal position, the agents that worked in the Northern District of Texas worked with the various DA's offices within their district. When an agent investigates a case that does not merit federal interest, the agent typically goes back to the State's prosecutor at the district level and requests that the State prosecute the case.

So, post-appointment, the agents on my detail were now full of questions about matters that I might be interested in as the new district attorney. I didn't have many answers yet, but I liked being part of the "campfire discussion" with the agents that were part of the detail.

I was starting to feel like the newly minted district attorney.

Chapter 17
Fifty: More Than a Birthday

MY BIRTHDAY, FRIDAY, the 12th of April, was a beautiful day. The weather was perfect, with no sign of rain. I was not going to accept the long-held belief that attaining the age of fifty for a woman meant you were old. I didn't feel that way. I felt ebullient.

It was a new beginning of a new chapter in my life.

My career plan had previously been to seek a higher bench and to move up through the judiciary. By taking this position as district attorney, that path had changed. I didn't know if I would ever sit as a judge again in a courtroom. But I would always have the experience of being a judge. The moniker of Judge was an honor I would always carry with me, even into retirement.

That Friday, however, I wasn't thinking about judging or prosecuting. I was thinking about celebrating. After all, it was my birthday, and a big one at that.

While Texas is known for its unbearable heat during the summer months, Texan springs are often lovely. I loved spring weather, particularly if we could avoid a thunderstorm or a tornado threatening the horizon. The humidity was below 50 percent and the day was warm, but not hot. The kind of day when bluebonnets, the legendary state flower, speckle the green spaces along the state highways.

Some of my friends had decided to leave work early and a celebration on a patio in Dallas was the first order of business to kick off the birthday festivities.

"LUCRETIA, I WASN'T sure you were going to make it!" I squealed.

I had regressed back to college, when Lucretia Shaw Scarth my college roommate arrived. Now she lived in Fort Worth and had made the drive over to Dallas for drinks on the patio at one of the city's many eateries.

"I wouldn't miss it!" she squealed in return, grinning. "I love you being a whole month older. I'm forty-nine. You're fifty," she reminded me. Her birthday was in May.

I was surrounded by a group of women that had been friends with me through the years. Lucretia was probably the oldest friend, going back to the '80s to our undergraduate days at Texas Tech.

Then there was Katherine. I grinned at her over my glass of wine. Our eyes locked. Katherine and I had known each other since law school at the University of Texas. The classes were so large that we did not meet at the law school campus, but at our mutual job. We both clerked for the Austin City Attorney's office and shared a desk while we researched legal issues. We later worked together at the Dallas County Criminal District Attorney's office and had remained friends over the years.

Katherine had shared in my losses and shared in the triumphs, too. Today was a triumph.

The group was rounded out with Sandra, Michelle, Mary, and Andrea, who were all successful businesswomen or judges in their own right.

"So, how is this going to work?" Andrea asked. "You really going to accept this appointment? You know we need to talk." She was emphatic. "Don't take it."

Andrea was concerned about my safety. She had expressed it before. I hadn't had a chance to explain Aaron's and my shared logic about being even safer. To her, I was an African American woman and I was making myself a target. She hadn't even thought I should apply and certainly shouldn't consider accepting the appointment.

"Seriously, you need to consider the risks," she said, her eyes narrowing, her face composed in a no-nonsense expression. I heard her, but I didn't want to discuss the negative aspects of being district attorney. I couldn't tell her that I had said yes and I was going to be the next district attorney in Kaufman, pending a senate confirmation hearing.

The conversation moved on to different topics: our work, the kids, and the security detail. No matter how macabre the reasons were to have a security detail, it was still pretty cool to have your own ensconced bodyguards.

The agents seemed to enjoy being outside, despite the small spectacle we were beginning to make. They had dressed for the occasion. Instead of wearing their normal slacks and loose shirts, tonight they had on suits, which dressed up their appearance and still concealed their weapons. I'm sure the patrons of the restaurant wondered who we were—was one of our entourage a famous entertainer, celebrity, or high-ranking political official?

"I want that one," Michelle said, grinning and pointing to one of the agents in hushed tones.

She had used her index finger to indicate one of the Homeland Security agents who looked exceptionally handsome in his dark suit. He was tall with dark hair, mirrored glasses, and a patient smile.

"I'm sure he heard you," I said. "That was a pretty loud whisper."

"Umm, that's okay," Michelle said, flashing another smile his way.

She was a beautiful woman and also one of my few unmarried friends. She was the type of woman that always got a second look from men. She could probably always have a boyfriend if she wanted to, but sometimes with her independence and work schedule, she would rather go it alone. She was a fierce competitor in the gas pipeline safety business, working for a small nonprofit company in our county. Her focus was primarily on school buses and children's safety, where the school buses cross path with gas pipelines throughout the country.

While our friendship had not been a long one, I appreciated her know-how and no-nonsense personality. For instance, when she learned that I was donating a kidney to my husband, she contacted the local media. In her business, she had contacts in the media and she didn't mind making calls. I was surprised that *The Dallas Morning News* wanted to do a story about the unlikely circumstance of a husband-and-wife match, and that the gift was given on Valentine's Day in 2008.

Returning to the present, I was starting to relax. The wine, conversation, my girlfriends, and a patio . . . that had the desired effect. My smiled widened.

"It isn't so bad being fifty," I mused to myself.

I looked up, and caught the eye of one of the men in the detail. He smiled at me briefly, then continued to cautiously scan the area surrounding the restaurant.

My thoughts traveled again to how much gratitude I had for these men and women who were here for us. I had begun to know and like the people on the detail, but I knew they had been pulled off other assignments to protect me and my family and the other officials in our county. I knew there was other law enforcement work to be done and I knew that in another week, we would have to reassess the threat level.

Would they be allowed to stay or would they go? If they stayed, it was more interruption to my life, but my family and I would be safer. However, the security detail's other assignments would continue to get pushed to the back.

These men and women were well-trained Homeland Security agents. When they left Kaufman County, how much danger would we all be in?

My smile faded. I felt the tension creep into my shoulders and the unanswered concerns return to the forefront of my mind. That was the problem with this case: we didn't have a suspect in custody, yet we all thought we knew who the suspect was.

We knew it was Eric Williams.

"There's something posted on Facebook about the case," Michelle said, interrupting my thoughts. Her phone, like the rest of ours, was laid on the tabletop, within easy reach.

We all knew what she meant when she said "the case." There was only one case on our minds.

"Judge, I just got a text too," Katie said, looking up from her phone.

And then, like on a television show, the TV over the bar across the patio interrupted regular broadcasting with a live news report.

"Kaufman County officials are executing a search warrant at the home of former Justice of the Peace Eric Williams at his residence in Kaufman. Sources have confirmed that the search is related to the recent murders in Kaufman County at the home of the Criminal District Attorney and his wife," the voice said from the broadcast.

The reporter continued, but for me the rest was white noise. I looked around at my friends gathered for my birthday celebration and snapped back to life.

"Oh my God!" I said. "This may be ending. I don't know what is going on, but they've got something."

No one knew what was going to happen next in the investigation, but the women surrounding me knew as I did that the threat was suddenly reducing before our eyes. There was a mental sigh. Was it too soon to express relief? I glanced at the agents. Their phones were getting texts, which meant that law enforcement was receiving credible information, not just news reports.

I figured they had more information about the new turn of events than I did, but I didn't ask. I didn't want to compromise anything by asking them what they knew. Did they seem more relaxed too, or was it my imagination? Was that ease from the news accounts or some other information they had learned from their contacts?

Either way, the party began in earnest. My friends, with security in tow, made another stop in Dallas. The evening was capped off with dinner at the famous Rosewood Mansion on Turtle Creek. With the fine weather and a beautiful view, the patio's offering was too much to resist. We shared dinner and when the evening ended, the detail returned us safely back home. My friends enjoyed the VIP treatment and the agents enjoyed the fact that probably for the first time since their assignment started, the actionable threat level had decreased.

The suspect would be in custody soon.

Later, I learned that the search of Eric Williams's home tied the anonymous email tip back to him. The previous week when Sheriff Byrnes had shared the tip with the judges, we all had a hunch it came from Eric Williams, but now they had evidence found in the search that tied him conclusively to the threat in the email—the number from the tip scrawled on a piece of paper next to Williams's computer.

The evidence still did not rise to the level of capital murder charges, but the email from Williams did meet the legal criteria of a terrorist threat. It wasn't much, but it did amount to something officials could hold him for while the investigation continued.

That weekend, the case against Williams built quickly. A friend of his came forward the following day and told police that he had rented a storage unit for Williams in Seagoville, Texas, a suburban city between Kaufman County and Dallas. Based on that information, another search warrant was executed. Law enforcement officials found a cache of weapons, a getaway car in the storage unit, and a single, unspent bullet that would ultimately tie him to Mark's murder too.

The net was closing in on Eric Williams.

Chapter 18
De-Robed

ON DAY FIFTEEN of the detail, the federal agents met with the Immigration Customs Enforcement supervisor and determined that the threat as it existed two weeks prior had lessened. They, after getting my input, agreed that despite the detail's initial twenty-one day assignment to protect my family and me, they should be relieved of their obligation due to Eric Williams's detention.

Although they had Williams in custody on a different charge, authorities knew they had the right man for the McLellands' murders. Now, everyone felt that it was simply a matter of time before they would be able to connect Williams to Mark Hasse's murder too.

With Eric Williams in custody, I was sure police would question his wife, Kim. Without her husband there to coach and give her mock support, I believed she would cooperate or at least be advised by her attorneys to cooperate with the special prosecutors. Once the net started to tighten, it would be too much for her to remain stoic and silent. Either way, I suspected she had to have knowledge of her husband's participation in the three murders. There is no way that you can live with someone and not know.

My suspicions were confirmed when Kim Williams was questioned. To most observers it was shocking, the level of her participation. I always suspected that she was more than the weak, drug-addled halfwit that many courthouse people believed her to be, but even I was surprised that she was the getaway driver in both crimes.

The Williamses had put their "kill game" into action and become a modern-day Bonnie and Clyde: by Kim Williams's account, it seemed that she had taken criminal action right alongside her husband. He would not have been as successful in his crimes if he had to commit the murders and then drive away from the scenes as well.

Besides the investigation, the appointment for District Attorney was heating up. After twenty-one days, the interim appointee would need to be replaced by the appointed DA. That deadline was fast approaching. Even though I had won the governor's support for the appointment, I still needed the Senate to act on the appointment through confirmation.

On Wednesday, April 17, 2013, Darrell Davila delivered the news I was waiting to hear: I had received Senate confirmation. State Senator Bob Deuell, who represented District Two and consequently Kaufman County, moved for consent of my appointment of the Kaufman Criminal District Attorney. State Senator Royce West, a Democrat from a Dallas district, joined him. It was nice to have a second from across the aisle, meaning confirmation from both Republicans and Democrats. That bipartisanship agreement proved to everyone that I had earned this appointment.

Senator West and I had been longtime associates. In my early years as a prosecutor in Dallas, he'd offered advice freely about the practice of law and some of the pitfalls that could befall young prosecutors making their way in legal practice. He was one of the first African American prosecutors hired in the later years of the former famous Dallas Criminal District Attorney Henry Wade, who held office for over thirty years, from 1951 to 1987.

Of course, Davila did not know about my history with Senator West. During our telephone call, he assured me that West's remarks on the Senate floor were warm and heartfelt, and that it was nice that my senator was joined by a Democrat with Senator West's gravitas. Furthermore, he told me I was unanimously confirmed by the entire Senate body.

Davila passed his congratulations along, but reminded me that the swearing-in needed to happen soon. I told him that between balancing my work schedule and organizing an impromptu ceremony, Monday, April 22 would be the earliest date we could do it. He agreed, and I set out to meet the deadline.

I had friends from our local women's group offer to prepare the snacks for the swearing-in ceremony. We anticipated that since there was no time for invitations and no one knew about the swearing-in, except by word of mouth, the crowd would be no more than fifty people. We anticipated friends, family, local officials, and organizations to attend

After the senate confirmation hearing, the rest of that week flew by.

Before I left on Friday for the weekend and my last official week as a judge, Katie and I put together a program for the swearing-in ceremony. It would open with prayer from Monsignor Duffey, an affable priest at Saint Martin of Tours, my local parish in Forney. Everyone loved him. He usually joked, even in his homily, and he was great with children. As he preached, he usually quizzed some of the kids on Biblical facts. Correct answers often earned them five bucks from his own pockets. This meant that the kids usually sat on the front row and tried to answer his questions. It was a great way to get them engaged in their faith.

After Monsignor opened in prayer, Katie's eight-year old daughter Gracie would lead the Pledge of Allegiance. Gracie was excited to have the chance to lead the pledge in front of a crowd besides a group of second graders. Judge Chitty would then make some personal remarks. Finally, Chief Justice Carolyn Wright of the Texas 5th Court of Appeals would swear me in. She was a professional associate and mentor to many women. She always had time to lend support to a fellow woman. She had agreed on short notice to attend and do the honors. Chief Justice Wright was a formidable presence. She rarely entered a room without you knowing she was there. Her presence, demeanor, and voice all commanded respect. And she deserved every bit of it: Chief Justice Wright had made her mark on Texas history by becoming the first African American woman to serve on the 5th Court of Appeals. I felt honored that she had made the time to swear me in.

Meanwhile, that weekend was the first one without my detail, or my shadows as I've often jokingly referred to them. It seemed like they had protected my family and me for a lifetime, but in fact it had only been fifteen days. I missed them individually, but I also enjoyed the freedoms that I had not had in a couple of weeks: going outside and walking the dog; running errands without making the security detail aware of my plans; and just getting to be spontaneous again.

Most importantly, it felt liberating to not have to worry that my would-be assailant would confront my security detail in the middle of night or in the early morning hours, like he had with the McLellands. I knew it was irrational, but sometimes I had wondered whether the person would want to go out in a "blaze of glory" and try to use my home and children as the instruments of that plan.

I thank God that we were never tested that way.

Despite all that, I tried to push my appointment and the case to the back of my mind. I had some personal family matters that had been on hold for weeks, like visiting my elderly aunt, who lived in Garland. I further had emails and texts from concerned friends and relatives to answer, and was in the midst of preparing for Brad's graduation.

Graduation was less than a month away and the invitations hadn't been sent. To be honest, they had not even been prepared. Even though eighteen-year-olds can easily do this themselves, it seems that the responsibility of stuffing and addressing invitations, buying and stamping envelopes, is often shared equally by mother and graduate.

We were also in the beginning throes of high school baseball playoff season. Jacob, who was a sophomore, needed some attention. Among other things, he was bitter about his sophomore baseball year. At the beginning of spring practice, he broke a finger, which took him out of play for the season. (Who knew a pinky finger could do all that?) I needed to get him back to the orthopedist to make sure he was released for summer baseball.

Yes, my job was all consuming—that a murder suspect was hunting me and my family was still unbelievable—but being a mom never stopped.

So, with Katie's help, the preparations for the swearing-in were complete. She and I parted ways, sentimental about the upcoming changes, but hopeful about the future. With my plans in place, I once again focused on my family and their lives, relieved that the ceremony on Monday would be a quiet, local event and thankful to enjoy my first weekend without my security detail.

WHAT I HAD envisioned on Monday was not what I walked into at 9 a.m. on Monday morning. There were people coming in and out of my office. It was complete chaos.

"Judge, *D Magazine* is going to be here to cover the swearing-in," Katie said as I walked in.

Before I could answer she rushed on.

"I got a call from the Dallas DA's office," she said, ushering me into my office and closing the door. "Heath Harris, the first assistant, is trying to confirm the time. He says that they are coming. Michelle Stambaugh (the head administrative assistant for the Kaufman County Criminal DA's office) wants to know if she needs to get the attorneys' affidavits prepared. All the ADAs need to be sworn in after you. Angie (the County Judge's secretary) wants to know if she needs to get the bond prepared for you, for the District Attorney, because your judge's bond for you now will be insufficient once you are no longer a judge. My phone has been ringing nonstop." She finally breathed and then added, "I think we are going to have a crowd."

Once she finished, I opened my mouth to speak, but Scott Smith, my court reporter, stuck his head into my office. The hallway was buzzing and Katie's office was starting to fill up with people needing information about the swearing-in.

"Judge, I called from my office, but no one here picked up," Scott said, glancing at Katie.

"I'm a little busy here," she snapped back, pointing to the obvious chaos of her office.

Now, Scott is a gentleman. His appearance is always that of a mature, well-dressed man. He possesses a skill set that is lamentedly outdated for men in Texas state courtrooms. He was a male court reporter who had come out of retirement to report for me after my former court reporter resigned to spend more time with her children. Scott had the opposite problem—with time on his hands, he realized he might have retired too soon from the Dallas courts. So this position had been a perfect fit for him.

"Hey Katie, I'm not judging you," he said. "It's a mess out there. The hallway is milling with people. Some people thought the swearing-in was at 10 this morning, instead of 1:30 this afternoon. I'm still trying to figure out how they even knew about it."

"I have no idea," Katie said, looking at me.

"I don't even have a Facebook and you know I didn't send out invitations, or rather, you didn't," I said, hands raised in the air, a common motion indicating surrender. "This is strictly word of mouth. Who knew this would happen?!"

Scott returned to the subject he came into the office about.

"I've got voice messages on my machine from seven different people asking about the swearing-in and wanting to know the time," he said. "What do you want me to do?"

I sprang into action, ticking off a list.

"Scott, go through your phone messages," I said. "Use your best judgment, but for the most part, anyone that wants to come to my swearing-in, I'm honored for them to be there. I will be the Kaufman County Criminal DA in a few hours and if they want to show support, it's a good thing. I'm going to need it. This isn't a secret ceremony. It will happen right here in my courtroom. Based on the number of calls that have been coming to you and Katie, we may have to come up with some more food. Katie can you order some trays from Brookshire's (the local grocery store)? We'll take anything. Get some for the reception and something for here in the office. I don't think we are getting lunch today. Can you get the sandwiches or do we need to get someone else to pick them up? When do you have pick up Gracie from school?"

"Let me make some calls," Katie said, smiling. "Brookshire's can usually make it happen if I can call them before 10. I'm picking Gracie up around noon. I need time to change her clothes out of her school uniform and tidy up her hair. I've got my curling iron. I can touch you up, too, Judge."

"I'll clear the hall," Scott said, interrupting the conversation. "I will let people know to come back at 1:30, for the big event," he finished, with a quick wink.

"My new bond, the ADAs' affidavits—is there anything else that we haven't thought about?" But before Katie could answer my question, I continued, "You mentioned that the other County offices are calling about getting some of the paperwork in order, let them do it."

"I've got it, Judge," she said, still smiling. "Just wanted to make sure with you before I called them back. By the way, Scott, Judge, there is a guy in the hall with his attorney. They're from out of town. The defendant wants to plead guilty and accept the State's offer. They are not set today. Nothing is set today, but it is a case assigned to this court. Do you want me to tell him to come back?"

She knew the answer.

"Of course not," I said.

I glanced at my watch. It was almost 9:30. I looked at Scott.

"Can you be ready to take a record by 10?" I asked.

It may be the last plea I take, I thought.

"Sure, that works," Scott said.

I turned to Katie.

"Call the DA's office upstairs," I said. "Make sure there is a DA available to sign him up for the plea and that they are in agreement."

"I can do that, Judge," Katie said.

I looked at them. My eyes misted.

"I'm going to miss you guys," I said, my voice cracking.

Neither one would make eye contact with me. I knew Katie's eyes were dewy. She had been that way for the last couple of days, but Scott's eyes were moist now, too. He ducked his head and went out of the door before I could confirm my suspicions.

FROM NOON ON, events were a blur. My friends, family, and work colleagues were unbelievable in their support. After the morning confusion, things happened as if they had been perfectly planned.

My husband arrived along with other family members, including the kids, my dad, my aunt, and some of my cousins from nearby Dallas. The noise from the hallway gradually grew in volume. The fifty people we anticipated had grown to almost two hundred guests. Among the number were judges (county, state, and appellate), DAs from surrounding counties, Texas state senators and representatives, and throngs of attorneys and other well-wishers.

D Magazine and the local media, along with a photographer and the publicity chair of the Kaufman County Republican Women's organization, all wanted to document this event. It was a big deal for the women of Dallas. In fact, media kept calling it landmark. I was awestruck. I never thought that there would be such interest in me accepting this position.

The photographer from *D Magazine* snapped pictures and interviewed both me and Aaron. We promised *D* that when the swearing-in was over, we would go downstairs for an impromptu photo shoot in the courthouse basement.

Chief Justice Wright arrived and ironed out details I had not thought about. Before the ceremony, she made me sit down with her, gather my thoughts, and become aware of the magnitude of the moment that was going to happen in a few minutes. The enormity of what had happened in Kaufman County and that the position that I had accepted had drawn the attention of the state and perhaps the nation.

"Judge," she said. "Erleigh, you are going to be the first judge I have ever de-robed and it will be my pleasure." She paused, and then continued, "I want you to know that I am proud of you. I remember you as that young DA in Dallas and now here you are. You will become the first female African American Criminal District Attorney in the state of Texas. Not that I'm surprised."

I knew she was trying to put me at ease. Nonetheless, I was privately speaking with one of the most powerful judges in the state. Without a doubt, she was the highest-ranking African American female jurist in the state at the time.

Then, it was 1:30. It was time.

Chief Justice Wright and I walked out to stand on my bench together. To accommodate the two of us standing on the judge's platform, the chair where I usually sat had been removed from the bench.

What I saw when I walked into my courtroom shocked me: the turnout was unbelievable! While I knew that Katie had said there was a growing crowd, it was still more people than I expected. My courtroom was filled beyond capacity. The small local swearing-in had turned into a spectacle. It was standing room only, and viewers had spilled out into the hallway and down the corridor of the courthouse. Someone had added seating in the well of the court, where the attorneys and defendants normally stood in front of the bench. The jury box was full.

I stood behind Chief Justice Wright when we walked out on the bench to begin the ceremony. She must have sensed my uneasiness, because when I joined her to stand beside her on the platform, she grabbed my hand.

I didn't hesitate: I took it and I held on.

| PART THREE |

Chapter 19
To Recuse or Not to Recuse?

RECUSAL WAS ONE of the first issues that I had to handle after getting sworn in. Would my District Attorney's office recuse itself from the Williamses' capital murder cases as the prosecutors on the case?

That was a decision that only the District Attorney could make. A classic example would be a DA employee or family member getting charged with a criminal matter; the DA's office would recuse themselves, but a court cannot force a prosecutor to remove themselves.

After Hasse's death, former DA McLelland recused himself, citing a "conflict." At the time of that decision, Hasse's murder was under investigation, but the investigation did not lead to an arrest.

People close to McLelland said that he had always felt Eric Williams was the suspect. He had not been happy at the direction the investigation had taken. He never felt it was the Aryan Brotherhood, or a Mexican cartel, or some other random, errant individual whom Mark had prosecuted years before.

In discussing the merits of recusal, I thought it was important to talk to one of the smartest people I knew in the criminal arena: Sue Korioth.

"I don't know, Sue," I said. She is an appellate lawyer with thirty years' experience who worked in the Kaufman DA's Office. "Why do I have a conflict?"

I put a heavy emphasis on the word "I."

"I'm different than Mike McLelland," I said to her. "I know Eric Williams, but then again, I know a lot of defendants. I had nothing to do with the theft trial that McLelland and Hasse were involved in. I wasn't the DA at the time of the shootings of any of the victims."

Korioth was a board-certified appellate and criminal attorney, which meant she had substantial experience and specific training in both legal areas. Being double certified was no small accomplishment. She had been a "go-to attorney" and supervisor in Dallas in the Appellate Division when I first started at the Dallas DA's office in 1990. Supervising a major division in a metropolitan city is no small matter.

That said, people rarely questioned Korioth. I could tell she didn't like it now, but the tables had turned. I wasn't a new ADA—I was her new boss.

Her face was sincere and I didn't see any bias in her expression as I was trying to weigh her words, judging her experience against her personal feelings. I knew while I was a judge, she made no secret of her disdain for me and certain rulings that went against the DA's office. I also knew that she wanted her colleagues, Bill Wirskye and Toby Shook, to prosecute this case, but who did prosecute it was ultimately my decision.

"You have a conflict because you were potentially a witness in the theft case on punishment," she said. "Didn't Mark talk to you about that? And, more importantly—"

"Yes, he did," I said, cutting her off. Sometimes, she still addressed me like she was the supervisor and I was her employee.

"But in the end, Mark didn't think that me cutting Eric's pay vouchers for overbilling the county was worthy punishment evidence," I continued. "We knew that he wouldn't be the first attorney to do that (overbill the county for work performed). A potential witness, not called, doesn't make a conflict."

I looked into her bespectacled eyes. She was wise and she knew the law inside-out. Her experience with capital appellate work was unprecedented in the state of Texas, but I didn't trust her totally in this case. She had too much of a personal conflict.

"I was going to say," she started, uncrossing her clog-shod feet and pausing for thought. Sue was no-nonsense in her speech, as well as her appearance, always dressing for comfort. Though attractive, her beauty was plain and understated.

"I was going to say," she started again. "I think the biggest problem is the search warrant you signed," she said. "You signed the search warrant for Mike and Cynthia McLelland's house."

I looked back at her because truly, I hadn't thought about the search warrant, but I hadn't forgotten that day. I could hardly forget: someone almost got shot at my house on Easter Sunday over that search warrant.

Bringing myself back to the present conversation, I responded to her.

I wasn't following her logic. "Yes, I signed a search warrant for the McLellands' house," I said. "I legally don't think the search warrant was necessary. There is no one that would have standing to complain about the search, but that's what the sheriff likes to do. He believes better safe than sorry on his search warrants. So?"

"I don't think that you should be the judge signing a search warrant and then turn around and be the prosecutor, prosecuting the capital murder," she responded. "I think it is a conflict. You wouldn't know, you haven't done one of these before."

She was referring to prosecuting a capital murder case.

"Before this motherfucker gets the needle, there will be all kinds of shit thrown at the wall," she continued. "And we don't want him to be breathing because we had a DA who was the judge signing a search warrant."

Sue Korioth was known for her salty language and she had held off during her entire persuasive tirade, but I could tell she was at her wit's end. To her it was an easy call. For me, I realized that I wanted to personally prosecute Eric Williams. I knew he had killed two people because he felt slighted and that he had no compassion for Cynthia McLelland, whose only offense was being married to the DA. To him, she had simply been disposable, and I wanted to see him pay for his carelessness and apathy.

Korioth had finally said something that held the ring of truth, regardless of whether she personally liked me or not. It wasn't that Eric was a motherfucker. (Though that was true, too.)

It was the life that a capital murder case took on after the case was tried.

A person convicted of capital murder often took years to receive the death penalty. There was the automatic appeal to the Texas Court of Criminal Appeals, but then writs of habeas corpus could be filed in the state and federal systems, which would delay it more years. During that time, the law could change. New facts could come to light. The jurists of the courts could change. And unfortunately, the politics of the day played a part in capital murder post-conviction decisions. Every single aspect of the trial would then be examined and reexamined by a number of people. It frustrated citizens who believed in the death penalty and wanted the sentence carried out expeditiously.

And instigating those certainties and delay was the best hand that the defense attorney could play in a legal game if you represented a death row inmate. Delay and time were your two best friends. The courts were unwitting participants because they were examining a cold record—the trial court's record of testimony and evidence—years after the defendant's horrible crimes. Over all those years, victims get forgotten by all except those most intimately concerned.

I had always felt that our humanity called for this process of examining and exhausting every possible reason why the state should not put a convicted capital murderer to death. In the wake of these murders, I now had a small inkling of how family members might feel in these types of cases because I was running short on sympathy for Eric Williams. He had had none for Mark, Mike, and Cynthia.

"Okay, you've given me something to think about," I said, looking back at her. "I'll think about the recusal."

She knew she had made her point, so she stood up to leave. As she walked out, it struck me that before this conversation, I had thought writing was her strong suit. Now, I realized she could argue a point if necessary. She had given me something to think about.

I sat back in my office chair. This office was unfamiliar to me still. I had grown accustomed to my previous office, my judge's chambers. I had more quiet, more time to think in chambers. Before, as it was now, my office door was always open downstairs adjacent to my court, but I didn't have a lot of traffic coming in and out of my chambers and I had had Katie as a watchdog at my door.

In contrast, here an open door was met with the constant in and out of prosecutors, investigators, and staff. I knew that they were trying to please their new boss. Many of the staff members were unfamiliar to me; even though I had seen them at the courthouse for years, I did not really know them. Everyone was friendly, though a little guarded. I was going to have to work at gaining their confidence and trust.

I shifted gears back to the work at hand, putting aside the personnel issues. I clicked the Westlaw Next icon, which is a research tool. The app was on my iPad, and I searched for "District Attorney Recusal."

Article 2.07 of the Code of Criminal Procedure defines disqualification.

Not that. I clearly am not disqualified, but should I recuse? I thought as I scanned the statute.

I flipped to the next section: "An attorney for the State who is not qualified to act may request the court to permit him to recuse himself in a case for good cause and upon approval by the court, is disqualified."

So the question for me was did "good cause" exist?

HOURS LATER, I arrived back home. Jacob had gotten a ride home from school and Brad was still there, busy with senior year activities, so I was able to go straight home without making any stops. Dinner wasn't an issue that night because we had leftovers in the fridge.

With time to think, I sipped a glass a wine. In my quiet house devoid of kids, husband, and detail, I realized how much life had changed in a week. It had been just a week ago when I had an armed guard detail, unable to drive or be alone. Now, Eric Williams was behind bars and I was the DA. It had been an eventful week to say the least.

I sighed as I heard the garage door open. The quiet had passed.

I was in the kitchen waiting to see which man in my life turned the corner. I suspected it was my husband since I heard the roar of his motor as he gunned into the garage.

"Aaron, that you?" I called out. "Su'prised you're home early."

As he turned the corner into the kitchen, Aaron smiled. He had on one of his favorite suits, a blue Canali, and he knew he wore it well.

I had to smile back.

"Yeah, I left a little early," he said. "Called your office. You didn't answer. I was hoping to find you here."

He angled up on the barstool with his leg and sat beside me. He leaned over and planted a kiss.

"Glass of wine?" I asked.

"Where are the kids?" he returned, not yet taking the glass from me.

"No one else is home," I said. "Both are still at school or on their way. Jacob is getting a ride home and Brad . . . well, Brad is Brad."

We discussed the kids and how they were doing currently. It was our eldest son's senior year and he had gone from being a serious student to being plagued by senioritis in the last few months. In talking about the kids, we could speak in code and understand each other. So Aaron knew what I meant when I said "Brad was being Brad." It meant that school was over and Brad was somewhere probably goofing off with another classmate.

"Well, then, no wine," he said. "I've got a better idea."

He leaned back over to me. The kiss deepened.

"Hey, we need to talk," I said, detangling myself from his amorous attention. "I'll get you the wine. You need to cool off."

His look was strained, but I knew not to laugh.

"Uhh, this better be good," he grumbled. "We haven't had the house to ourselves—"

"I'd like your thoughts about me, or rather about the DA's office recusing itself," I said, interrupting. "I talked to Sue and she thinks 'good cause' exists."

I handed him the wineglass and made eye contact. His smile had definitely turned upside-down. I got up and poured the wine.

"It's the issue of the office recusal. Is there good cause for this office to recuse itself?" I asked, sitting the bottle of wine on the kitchen bar and popping back on the barstool beside him.

"I smell something that isn't right," he said. "Why do you need to recuse the office? You weren't a victim. You were a judge at the time of the murders."

He frowned as he scolded me. "I just think some folks want you out and a recusal would be the way to achieve that," he said.

"Some folks? Who are the 'some folks'?" I asked. "They all work for me."

"Just because they work for you . . . listen, last week, some people didn't like you as the judge," he said. "And now, they want to get rid of you doing this case so they can have their guys doing this case. You know: the ol' boys."

He fumed, doing air quotes when he said "ol' boys." Aaron often felt my slights more than I did, but I thought that Sue had a legitimate concern and he needed to hear it.

"Look, I know who liked and didn't like me before I took this job," I said. "People will adjust once they know I'm on their team, not a judge—or, in their opinion, a judge that didn't always rule for the prosecution. But Sue has a legitimate point about the search warrant that I signed the day after the murders."

I explained Sue's points to him. I would be wearing the judge's robe and the prosecutor's proverbial white hat in the same trial against Eric. Even though we agreed that it really didn't matter, we both knew that in a capital murder case, any issue large or small could be the difference between life in prison or an execution.

After a few more minutes of exchange as lawyers, not spouses, each making points about our position, Aaron finally halted the conversation.

"It really doesn't matter what I think," he said, looking at me squarely in the eyes. "You are going to do what you want to do. What you think is right. My problem is I don't like those guys pushing you around for their own purposes, but this is not about pride. This is about justice and there won't be justice if Eric Williams doesn't get the needle in the end."

Aaron wanted Eric to pay for his crimes, but he also wanted him behind bars for my safety.

"Come here," he said, leading me off the barstool and taking my hand. "I don't want to fuss. I can tell you've already made your mind up."

He had his eye on the couch.

"Let's sit down and quit talking about work," he said, taking the wine glasses and putting them on the coffee table. "And get back to where I was."

One arm was around my shoulder. The other arm and hand were inching back up my skirt, and he had clicked the TV on as he lounged back on the couch.

The man had skills.

"Mmmm," I hummed, murmuring against his lips as I began to relax. "Better than talking about work."

"Shh."

I was starting to feel that feeling that only Aaron made me feel. My mind began to float.

"Mom? Aaron?!"

The front door burst open. Jacob's ride had dropped him off and he'd used the front door and his key to come in instead of the garage door, meaning we didn't hear him.

"Damn!" Aaron muttered under his breath, sliding his hands back in place.

I stood up, smoothing out my skirt.

"In here, sweetie," I called out, looking down at Aaron. He had that pained look on his face again. This time, I had to laugh aloud.

"Laugh all you want," he said quietly, adjusting his face as Jacob rounded the corner into the kitchen and family room. "You are mine tonight."

"Come on and help me warm up some leftovers," I said to my son.

I walked into the kitchen, giving Aaron a moment alone. I realized when I stood up that he needed to adjust more than his face.

"Sure thing," Jacob said, slinging his school backpack on the floor.

Before he could start helping me, he had come up with a better idea.

"I think I hear Brad," he said, looking at me with hope in his eyes, as the garage door went up for the second time that evening. "Maybe we can take some grounders before dinner?"

"I got this," I said. "Go play with your brother while the sun is still out."

I smiled at him and waved him away with my hands. He was sixteen, but he and his brother were still kids. In the evenings after school, they sometimes played baseball in the front yard, throwing the baseball back and forth for hours.

Jacob had grown five inches from last year and he was slimming as he grew taller. He boasted a baseball player's build, as opposed to his brother, who was muscular and built like a running back. But they both loved the game of baseball.

As I warmed up our dinner, I glanced over at Aaron, who was watching the news. The kids were outside, and I could faintly hear the ball smacking their gloves as they shouted back and forth at each other.

I walked to the front door to call the kids in to dinner. The same door where the agents had rung the doorbell to ask me to sign the warrant. The same door that other officers came to when they came to my home on official business. It was where company came or people on business, not usually where family or close friends entered, unless the garage door was down.

My mind began to wander. *Would Eric have tried to come through this door, down the hall to me and Aaron's room or God, up the stairs to the kids' room? To make sure he would leave no witnesses, like he did with Cynthia? STOP!*

My brain shouted at me.

I knew Eric Williams didn't like me, but he hadn't wanted to kill me.

I shook my head as if to shake away the scary thoughts, but I still had that feeling.

That's Aaron making me feel like Eric wants to kill me. I don't know that.

I did the sign of the cross and squared my shoulders. I opened the door and yelled out to my children. "Hey, y'all need to come on in and eat. Dinner's ready."

I smiled, my thoughts calming down.

Everything is all right. At least it was that night.

Chapter 20
Special Prosecutors

SUE'S COLLEAGUES BILL Wirskye and Toby Shook had been appointed as special prosecutors when I officially made the decision to recuse the Kaufman County DA's office from the prosecution of Eric Williams. Sue Korioth had convinced me that being the Judge that signed the search warrant and later prosecuting the same case could potentially create a conflict. Moreover, the District Attorney's office had another unique conflict; never before in the history of this country had two members of the same DA's office (and one of their family members) been assassinated. While we were not the family members of Mike, Mark, and Cynthia, everyone in the District Attorney's office felt victimized by these murders.

As the new Criminal District Attorney, I also was faced with Mike McLelland's prior decision to recuse the DA's office when Mark Hasse had been killed in January 2013. Before Mike's untimely death, Mike had already determined that there was good cause for the office not to prosecute the murder of one of its former employees.

Enter Wirskye and Shook. Wirskye had been working nonstop on this case for the last few months leading up to the jury selection, which was scheduled for September 22, 2014. He and Shook had put together a trial team, combining state, federal, and volunteer resources. Everyone was eager to help. No one killed prosecutors and got away with it in Texas.

Essential to proving Williams's guilt and getting the death penalty, was getting his wife, Kim, "to flip," she had to tie her husband to Hasse's murder in the prosecutor's case-in-chief—the portion of the trial in which the prosecution presented its case—to the McLellands' murders in the punishment phase of the trial.

During her debriefing, Kim gave evidence of the crimes, which led the investigators to locate weapons and some of the other items of evidence that Eric Williams had tossed to the bottom of Lake Tawokoni.

She also named other potential victims, which proved to be a critical part of her testimony. If Eric Williams had not been caught by the police, he would have continued his killing spree. He would have made his way down that list to the next innocent person. That means he was considered a future danger. And that gets you the needle in the state of Texas.

Kim Williams had been portrayed by the media as an unwitting accomplice. I felt differently. She had lived with Eric and knew the people he hated. And the people he hated, she hated. His slights were her slights. They were married for twenty-one years and she enjoyed playing the "kill game" as much as he did.

The kill game was something she had bragged that she and Eric played together and it was just what it sounded like: planning the gruesome murders of people and how they could get away with it. Imagine a couple entertaining themselves with that game in the evening.

If I had previously doubted that recusing my office was the correct legal decision for the Kaufman District Attorney's office, when I learned I was one of the pawns in their twisted game during the spring of 2014, I knew that our office could not have tried that case. If our office had not recused in 2013, we would have discovered the evidence from Kim Williams months before the trial in 2014, which would have then clearly been reason to recuse, delaying the trial even more.

I learned about the kill list in April from Bill Wirskye. Bill was a giant of a man. He stood six foot eight. He had a pleasant face and an easy demeanor, unless you were a man charged with capital murder; then he was deadly serious. So, when Bill asked to speak to me privately in my office and shut my office door, I glanced up from my seat—it was no small distance. His face was grim. He was deadly serious.

"Bill, what's up," I said, as I began to rise to meet his gaze.

"Judge, why don't you sit down," he said, pointing to my chair.

"You are scaring me, what's up," I asked again. I was firmer and I still stood.

"Erleigh . . . sit down, I want to talk to you about something," he countered gently. Lowering his voice, as I slumped back into my sit.

He continued "We've been debriefing Kim. I can't tell you about her testimony, but I can tell you that there was a list."

". . . a list," I mumbled, interrupting Bill.

Bill continued, as if I hadn't spoken, "Yes, Eric Williams had a list, and your name was on the list."

The list was real. It may not have been written, but Kim and Eric knew who they were going to assassinate next. She said that Eric Williams planned to kill me and Judge Glen Ashworth. Bill didn't know the order and I don't know that it actually mattered.

Chapter 21
Another Capital

I HAD TO put the Williams case out of my mind for a while; we had competent special prosecutors to handle the capital murder cases. It was time to turn to the task that the governor had appointed me for: to start rebuilding the Kaufman County Criminal District Attorney's office. The office had been shaken by the three murders.

There were no easy summer days for me in 2013, the first summer I took over as District Attorney in Kaufman. I had some tasks that had to be completed in short order. First, we had to get back to prosecuting cases. Second, I had to go through the office policies and decide if there needed to be changes or whether to maintain the status quo. Mike had left files in his office that had been important to him, and ultimately I had to figure out my office personnel—who they were, what their goals were, and what made them tick.

The first two didn't take much time. The latter did. It was going to take time to build relationships.

There were thirty-two employees who worked for the District Attorney's office in Kaufman County at that time: thirteen attorneys (fourteen if you counted me), five investigators, and fifteen support staff.

The support staff was the heart and soul of the office. Most were certified paralegals. Others managed the running of other essential programs for the office, like collecting restitution for victims, managing the intake and disposition of cases, and, most importantly, coordinating with the victims and the families of the victims of crime.

Their relationships with me before I was appointed as their boss stemmed from the interactions they had with me as a judge. Beyond the attorneys in the office that prosecuted their cases in my court, I had no relationship with the other employees (investigators and paralegals). Their opinions of me had been based on what they had heard about me through the years. For instance, there were rumors circulating around the courthouse that I had accepted the job as DA only so I could run for District Judge in a few short months. Thinking that I was using their office to further my judicial career did not lend trust to an already tenuous relationship.

While I knew that I would not run for Judge, they didn't yet. So instead of throwing my name in for District Judge, I announced my intent to seek the position that I had been appointed to in the upcoming election: Criminal District Attorney of Kaufman County. The primary election would be held in March 2014 and the general election in November of the same year, but I wanted to announce early and did so in the summer of 2013 to dispel any myths that I might be running for another position. I knew this decision might cost me a future judicial career. Once you left the bench, going back was not always an option. But I had given my word and I planned on keeping it.

It was not until the end of the summer, when all of the Kaufman County DA's office employees were honored by Texas District and County Attorneys Association (TDCAA), that the office began to feel like my own. The annual conference was held in Galveston. Because we were being honored, TDCAA awarded the office tuition for the conference, which allowed more of the staff to attend. I only had to budget for travel and expenses for my office.

Leaving a skeleton crew behind, most of the employees traveled south for the week-long conference, which covered relevant legislative updates, investigative tools, and best workplace practices. It was the place to be for DA's offices throughout the state.

The award ceremony that the association hosted at the conference was touching, as the TDCAA staff reminded the hundreds of attendees how Mark Hasse and Mike and Cynthia McLelland were gunned down in the line of duty.

Rob Kepple, the executive director of the TDCAA, presented me with the Lone Star Prosecutor Award, the plaque of which was in the shape of the state of Texas. The award recognized prosecutors and their office personnel for advancing justice in their communities. Later, he sent smaller replicas to every member of the staff that was employed at the District Attorney's office at that time. It was a moving event.

After the formalities ended, the fun began. I shared meals with different members of the staff during various evenings. We swapped war stories with each other, remembering shared courtroom experiences.

I also learned more about their personal lives and began to get a better idea of who these amazing people were that worked with me. In turn, they got to know me better. Prior to this, they had only known me as a judge and as their boss. They had never seen me "let my hair down." Spending time with the staff away from the office let me do that. By the end of the week, I think I struck the right balance between professional and personal.

One of the more fun, but sober, evenings was with John Long, his wife Susan, and Aaron. John had been at the office for six years and through two previous administrations: three years with Mike McLelland and three years with Rick Harrison. Unlike other employees in the office, John had always seemed to understand that my role as judge, and now as District Attorney, would not be a conflict, but my prior position would enhance my position as his new boss. He knew that my style would be different than my predecessors and if there were any issues in the transition, that I could bridge those differences. John was quickly becoming a confidant. He was upbeat and positive and his manner belied the serious disease he lived with, colon cancer.

As he liked to say, I had gone from a referee to coaching the team. Without John, I don't know if my transition would have gone as smoothly.

So, in contrast to the casual, loud dinners that I had shared with the younger employees, John and I, along with our spouses, had a quiet meal. We shared dinner at an offbeat restaurant frequented by the locals of Galveston.

The night was balmy and breezy. The restaurant had a nice crowd, but it wasn't packed. We were seated by an attentive waiter whose suit's prime had passed. He looked as if he had been working at the restaurant for years. It was if we had stepped back a few decades in time with him. His manner and appearance were old-fashioned, as he handed out the menus and deftly removed our napkins from the tabletop to our laps. He knew the menu items and ran through his favorites with us. After taking his suggestions, we ordered. The food did not disappoint, and the company was exceptional.

We laughed through each other's standard "how-did-you-meet" couple conversation. John and Susan's story was funnier than Aaron's and mine. Theirs sounded like something out of a corny 1950s movie. They had gone on a double date and ultimately ditched their original dates, realizing they were made for each other. It was fun, and John and Susan played off each other as they shared the zany details.

As the evening came to a close, we sat at the table making light conversation. We were enjoying each other's company and the last morsel of a wonderful crème brûlée, when John broke the reverie of idle chatter.

"You know, Judge, I am going to continue to do the best job I can for you as long as I can," he said.

I wondered if I should pretend I didn't know what he was talking about. The evening had been fun and I did not want to bring the mood down, but I resigned it would be in poor taste to make light of a man that had terminal cancer by pretending to not understand what he meant.

We all knew that John was sick and he was fighting cancer again for a second time. He was fighting for his life.

"I know, John," I finally said. "You've already done a hell of a lot for me and I am not just talking about legal work. I'm talking about the way the kids saw me before I started the job and now. I had no idea I was known to be such a 'witch on the bench.'"

I smiled. We sometimes referred to the younger attorneys as the kids.

"They are young," he said, taking the compliment. "They just don't get it."

We both knew it just wasn't the younger staff, but some of the older members of the office as well. He continued on his earlier topic, not to be dissuaded.

"I'm feeling better and I have the best doctors," he said.

"John, you look great and I know as long as you feel like it, I can count on you," I said, reaching across the table to squeeze his hand.

I looked at Susan. Her eyes had misted. She nodded her head imperceptibly, as if to say, "Thanks."

"Okay, now explain to me again why you were so rude to Erleigh, Aaron, when she called you up for a date to a Mavericks game?" Susan said, lightening the mood. "Who wouldn't want to go to a Mavericks game?"

The moment had passed. I moved my hand off John's, where it had been lightly resting atop one of his on the table, and then grabbed Aaron's under the table.

Our conversation was trailing off. We looked around and realized we were the only remaining table in the restaurant. The night had been a good respite from the week.

I knew tomorrow would be different. It would be the last night at the conference, so the entire office would have dinner and meet afterwards for tropical drinks with funny umbrellas. It would be hot, loud, and fun. That's where the younger set liked to hang out, so I would be there. I smiled and thought that the conference had turned out better than I had expected.

After the conference that summer, the atmosphere at the office was better, more congenial. We were still working through the transition, but I was six months into the job. It was October and I made the mistake of thinking I was on top of things at the office, after the dog days of summer. Then, things changed.

CALLS IN THE middle of the night are almost never good.

As a parent with teenagers, you hold your breath when the phone rings at 2 a.m. You do a mental inventory of who is home and who isn't. Once you have mentally gone through those calculations, you start thinking about family members you could be getting a call about. The thoughts that run through your mind in those quick seconds before you get the person on the other end of the line are intense.

"Hello," I said, clearing my throat. I tried to sound as if I wasn't asleep, not realizing that on pre-dawn calls, no one expects you to be awake.

"Judge, this is Chief Lay, Terrell Police Department," the voice said. He sounded official.

My mind was still reeling. I was trying to put together fragmented thoughts and clear my head.

"I know who you are," I said reassuringly.

I had only been the DA for six months, but even I knew that the Chief of Police didn't wake up the DA in the middle of the night unless something was wrong.

"What's going on?" I asked.

"We've had a shooting in Terrell," he said. "To be exact, we've had seven shootings. Well, five fatalities that we expect are all homicides. There are no police officers hurt."

My mind had gone from fuzzy to fully alert.

I started where he had left off.

"No officers hurt," I said. "The crime scenes, how many are there?"

"There are three homicide crime scenes and another one we think may be related," he said. "We have secured the scenes. We have people collecting evidence at the scenes."

"And the suspect?" I asked.

"He's in custody, after a chase," Chief Lay said. "He bailed out in the woods, but we have him." He filled me in on some of the evidence they had collected at the crime scenes. He gave me the suspect's name and what they knew about him and his prior criminal record.

He breathed out, with what sounded like relief. He sounded exhausted.

"I'm going to try and get a few hours of sleep before the morning," he said. "It's been a long night."

"Yes sir, it has," I said. "Good work getting the suspect in custody."

I glanced at the clock that was atop Aaron's nightstand: it was almost 2:30 a.m. I hadn't realized that at some point in the conversation, Aaron woke up too. He must have heard my cell phone ring and sensed the urgency of the conversation.

"Chief, what time do you want to meet in the morning? Does nine work?" I asked.

We had a suspect, which meant we had a defendant. And that meant I had work to do. It looked like it would be for a capital murder case, if there were five victims.

"I will be at the DA's office at nine," he confirmed.

"That's fine," I said. "See you then." As I hung up, I heard him let out another long exhale. He sounded like it had been a long night.

Aaron had turned the light on. I clicked my cell off and turned back toward him. He had discerned most of the events from my one side of the conversation, but I filled him in on the details. It was hard to believe that while we slept, five people in our county had been murdered.

"Go back to sleep," I said. "I've got to make a few notes." My mind was still running.

"Do you need me to stay awake with you?" Aaron offered.

I leaned over and kissed him.

"Nah, get some rest," I said. "You've got court tomorrow. I'm fine. I'm just going to jot down a few notes."

"Okay," he said.

I got up and found my iPad on the desk. Chief Lay had told me the defendant's name, Charles Brownlow. I googled both Brownlow and Terrell, Texas. From CNN to the local media outlets, the news accounts jumped off the screen, reporting the story.

I found a pen and a legal pad. I started making notes as questions popped in my head. There were three crime scenes. The news stories reported that the shooter killed his mother, aunt, two friends, and a convenience store clerk and attempted to injure two others.

That's a crime spree.

I stood up and stretched, glancing at the clock. It was almost 5 a.m. I climbed back in bed, grabbed my phone and texted my first assistant: 5 people killed in Terrell. Suspect in custody. Office meeting with Chief Lay at nine. See you there. ENW.

I lay down, closed my eyes, and waited for sleep to overtake me, but it didn't come. My mind was fully engaged. My thoughts moved from the case to my job as DA and how different it was from the bench.

I had been awakened many times before for a warrant, but even after reading some of the unpleasant facts of an affidavit, I could go back to sleep. As the judge, my only job was to determine probable cause. Unless the case ended up in my court, I never thought about it again.

Being the DA was completely different.

The case was mine the whole way: from investigation, to trial, to sentence, to appeal. I tried to slow my mind down. I breathed in and then let out a long exhale.

I thought I sounded like Chief Lay, when he got off the phone with me earlier, issuing that same long exhale. By now, I didn't have to look at the clock to figure out the time. I knew what time it was. Night had become morning. It was time to get up.

Chapter 22
Pre-Trial

THE WEEKS LEADING up to Williams's trial were more emotional for my office than I could have imagined. I knew about PTSD and understood the concept, but I didn't realize until the trial neared that many members of my office staff suffered from the condition, in varying stages.

As the Thanksgiving holiday ended, I sat in my office with Michelle Stambaugh. She was the office manager and the heart of the office. Therefore, I went to her to try to get an opinion of how the office staff was emotionally handling the upcoming trial.

"Judge, I know the girls are trying to work, but they are distracted," she said.

We were discussing the lowered productivity among the support staff, which the attorneys had complained to me about, and I had subsequently brought the concern to her.

"I know," I said. "I just didn't realize how affected they would be with the trial approaching."

"I know, but it's real. I feel it too," she said. Hesitatingly she began, "I think it will help, I mean, I'm glad that since there is a live feed of the trial, we will be able to watch the trial. That is, if you don't mind?"

I had thought about the trial feed before Michelle even brought it up. In fact, I'd already discussed it with the County's IT chief, George York.

George loved technology and could easily go on and on after you asked basic computer questions. I knew how to turn on my computer, check my email, and use Microsoft Word to draft documents. After that, everything else was a mystery to me.

Not so for George. He had explained to me that since there was a television cable coming from the courtroom live, we just had to get permission from the network to access the feed. They were already allowing a viewing of the court trial outside of the courtroom. In anticipation of the overflow of court watchers, newspaper journalists, and media reporters, there would be a room set up carrying the trial.

"I don't want them watching the trial all day," I said. "They've got to work. But on their breaks, if they want to watch it, they have to do it at their desks, with ear plugs. I'm not blasting the trial on the televisions in the office."

I paused for a beat, and then went on.

"Besides, I don't want to hear it and I shouldn't because I could be called as a witness," I said. "And I think it may be unnerving for other people that don't want to hear the trial."

"Agreed," Michelle said. "Thanks, Judge."

As she stood to leave, I really looked into her face and realized that this was really hard for her too.

As the heart and soul of the office, Michelle had been a rock for the staff since the murders happened. After their boss and his wife were killed, she was the point of contact for all DA office employees. Michelle had sent text messages about breaking news; made sure to account for office personnel to law enforcement; and kept in touch with all DA personnel during those first scary days of uncertainty. Ultimately, on the day of Mike's funeral, she'd driven the entire office over en masse to his funeral services in her church's bus.

I could only imagine her wielding a bulky church bus, full of grief-stricken ADAs, investigators, and paralegals, with her slight frame. That image stuck in my mind just then, making my heart full and my throat dry.

Not only had Michelle kept the office together, but she had assisted the victim-witness coordinator with victim services. Victim services are exactly what it sounds like: aid for victims. It consists of a coordinator who works behind the scenes offering services to the family of victims while the attorneys are getting cases ready for court. In some ways, trials function like any other production. Outwardly one only sees the players in the courtroom, such as the judge, the lawyers, and the witnesses called to testify. However, it's people like Shirley Bruner, the victim coordinator, with the help of someone like Michelle, who work to get the witnesses to court and find accommodations for them while they are waiting to testify.

Even though this case was being tried by other lawyers and another judge in an adjacent county, Kaufman County had assisted in coordinating with the victims with their questions, concerns, and needs leading up to the trial. The costs were paid by the state of Texas, but the County had to initially make the accommodations and pay the costs and await the state's reimbursement for the victims' families.

Our office had contacted the McLellands' family, assisting them with travel arrangements, once we were certain that the trial date was firm. As we got closer to the trial date, we were glad to get their calls, as they had questions about logistics about the upcoming trial. Our office had gotten particularly close to Mike's sons and daughter.

"Are you okay?" I asked Michelle, coming out of my reverie, as I realized she was still standing and looking at me expectantly.

"I'm going to be okay," she said. "I just want this behind us. I can't ever feel too bad for the office because I just remember Mike and Cynthia's families . . . and I know how hard it must be for them. They lost their mom, dad, son, daughter, sister."

She didn't finish as she choked on the last words, thinking about their losses.

AS 2013 ENDED with another capital murderer in Kaufman County awaiting trial, I realized that in the last year, I had been in contact with capital murderers more than I could have ever anticipated in my career.

I was preparing to prosecute one accused of killing five people, including his mother. I had learned that another hated—and planned to assassinate—me. Ultimately, I discovered I would have to testify in the trial against the killer of my colleagues in the punishment phase of the trial, where prosecutors were seeking the death penalty. The last part of my "capital murderer trifecta" came in the form of the conversation I had with Bill Wirskye. Looking back, I realized that conversation was pivotal for me; up to that point, I never fully comprehended that Eric Williams wanted to kill me and that he would have acted on his hate.

Don't get me wrong—I knew he had killed three people.

Still, my mind rejected that heinous thought, as it related to me: that I was supposed to be next.

Up until then, I denied the truth that, in Aaron's astute observation, I was always one of Eric Williams' targets, since he would not stand for me telling him what to do. I ignored my husband's warning that a man like Williams was not ashamed of his bad behavior—cheating the county out of money for work he didn't do—and that he would see me as an intermeddler, a judge overstepping her boundaries.

For all my hesitation in accepting the reality that Eric Williams hated me with a murderous passion, now I knew that it was true. His wife had no reason to lie about that. She divulged the "hit list" that she and her slaughtering husband created with the dispassionate, detached ease of someone ticking off sightseeing attractions on their summer vacation.

As my mind turned that thought over again and again, I realized how naïve I had been. I realized suddenly that we try to explain away most people's criminal behavior. We look at their rough childhood, their bad parents, and their prior criminal behaviors.

Sometimes, it makes sense.

But then we see another person who was a bed-wetter, or had horrible parents, or dropped out of high school. That person doesn't turn into a serial murderer.

Williams was an anomaly. He'd set out to collect victims because of some perceived injustice or grievance. He had twisted his wrongdoing into some public service he was doing for the county. He never accepted that he stole from either his overbilling of county services —or, later, computer equipment—and that the job he was doing was something any competent attorney with integrity could do.

The psychopathic malignancy that Eric Williams embodied would have to be explained by a highly trained professional.

To me, he personified pure evil.

I knew I had brushed shoulders with the devil. I felt that the Lord, like in Exodus, had allowed evil to pass over my family and me, leaving us untouched.

Chapter 23
It Begins

ON DECEMBER 4, 2014, the guilt phase of Eric Williams's capital murder trial began. A criminal trial in Texas consists of two parts. The prosecutors have to prove that the defendant is guilty and only then would they be allowed to put on punishment evidence in the penalty phase. If a jury of twelve found him guilty, the special prosecutors for Kaufman County would seek the death penalty.

From the outset, I had been vocal about not listening to the evidence. I held fast to that decision and refrained from tuning in. I have a thumb drive of the trial that was given to me after the trial by George, should I ever care to listen.

From time to time in the office, I would see the faces of people as they listened to or watched the trial proceedings. Their faces seemed to vacillate between astonishment, sadness, and jubilance. I could only assume that they had heard evidence from the testimony that they had not expected; evidence that was surprising, or sad, or made them feel that the special prosecutors were making a good case in front of the jury.

The pace of work getting done around the office had gone from slow to a grinding halt. Everything save cases being filed took second place to the trial.

All eyes were on Eric Williams. The people of Kaufman County waited and wondered what his fate would be.

Thankfully, we did not have to wait long. On Thursday, December 8, the jury found Eric Williams guilty of capital murder. The judge recessed the case and pronounced that the punishment phase of the trial would start the next Monday.

Everyone's mood in the DA's office almost instantly lightened. The office seemed to let out a collective sigh of relief. Even though most people assumed the jury would convict him, one could never tell which direction a jury would go.

We all knew the stakes were much higher for punishment, but the atmosphere around the courthouse and the county in general felt like the fourth quarter of your hometown football game once the home team was sure to win. At this point, though, we could not afford a single fumble, interception, or turnover. We needed to play it all the way out, without errors.

Conventional wisdom in legal circles held that now the trial was in the State's favor. If the jury found Eric Williams guilty in the guilt phase based only on the McLellands' case, then when the jurors heard all the other evidence, they would have enough evidence to give him the death penalty.

The decision would be hard.

Having never participated in a capital murder prosecution, I did not know that this experience would affect me personally. I had thought about my feelings about capital offenses and the punishments it involved. I had thought about the law in Texas and what the District Attorney's office would or could do if a person committed a criminal act that made him or her eligible for the death penalty. But to be selected to be part of a jury and to make the decision to end someone's life was different. Similarly, to be called to testify and know that something you witnessed could help convince a jury that death was the righteous outcome seemed a heavy burden to bear.

Every attorney I spoke to who had completed a capital case and every training I had ever attended in my career had emphasized the challenge of the punishment part of the trial, where you had to ask the jury for the ultimate sentence—death. The verdict on that remained unanimous: for attorneys, witnesses, and jurors alike, it is a life-changing experience.

As the week closed out, I started to think that I would escape that responsibility of testifying. That somehow, it would simply bypass me because they wouldn't need my testimony.

The Regional Public Defenders, the attorneys appointed to represent Eric Williams, had called and subpoenaed the staff in my office, courthouse personnel, and attorneys who had worked with Eric Williams. They were gathering defense evidence to present to the jury in the punishment phase about the relationships the defendant had with people in the community.

Their goal? To find any potential witnesses who could mitigate the pivotal issue of "future danger." Surprisingly neither his father, nor his sister were called to plead for his life. Their testimony was double-edged. His father couldn't take the stand because of his former white supremacist ties and his sister knew of his merciless animal killing as a child. Not surprisingly, I had not received a call from the public defenders.

But I did receive a call from Toby Shook.

"Hey Judge, this is Toby," he said.

"Yes, I recognize your voice, Toby," I said. "How are you?"

"Tired, missing my family," he said matter-of-factly. "But this is what we do."

Part of the special prosecution team, Shook shared a criminal defense practice with Bill Wirskye. They were both former Dallas County prosecutors. After Wirskye was appointed to the Mark Hasse case, Shook was soon added. Everyone knew that the State could only benefit from his legal expertise.

Shook was the stuff of legend at the Dallas County DA's office. Former District Attorney Judge Vance had hired him in the late 1980s. When I started in the Dallas DA's office in 1990, I had no idea then why people revered him so, but it soon became apparent even to a newly licensed Texas "baby lawyer" with the ink still wet on her law degree and bar license.

Vance had tasked Shook with disposing of old criminal cases that had been "gathering dust" in the DA's office during the last years of the Henry Wade dynasty, the famous Dallas District Attorney who was the longest serving prosecutor in the country. Wade was made famous not only for his breadth of service, but for his involvement in the prosecution of Jack Ruby who assassinated Lee Harvey Oswald and being designated as the named defendant in the renowned *Roe v. Wade*.

When Shook was tasked with disposing of cases, that meant pleading cases or even dismissing those that could no longer be proven because witnesses were no longer available. Other times it meant doing what Shook did best: trying the hell out of cases, even if they were colder than a polar bear's nose and no one expected him to win.

As if cleaning up Dallas's cold cases were not enough, Shook proved his mettle with his work on the infamous Texas Seven case. In December 1999, when the Texas Seven escaped from the Connally Unit, a maximum-security south Texas prison, Shook's prosecution of those escapees solidified his place in Texas history.

So getting a phone call from Shook, in this context, felt surreal; suddenly, here we were on odd ends of a capital murder trial together.

"I need to talk to you about next week—" he said.

"By the way, thank you," I said, interrupting him. "I heard you guys did a good job."

"No thanks necessary," he said. "It was Bill. Bill has been on this since the beginning. He is lead. It's him and the whole team," he added modestly. Then he pivoted to the reason for the call. "But now, Judge, we got to think about punishment."

He quickly brought the conversation back to the point of his phone call. Time was of the essence.

"Okay," I said.

"Judge, I told you we might need you in punishment and we do," he said. "We are going to put you on the witness stand in punishment. We want the jury to have a name with the face, from Eric's list. You understand . . . future danger . . ."

His words pushed me into stunned silence. I knew this was possible all along, but I prayed it would not come to this.

I guess I was silent too long.

"Erleigh?" Toby asked.

"I'm here," I said, my voice faltering. "I know you said you might need me to testify. I just didn't realize that you really would."

Sensing my unease, he changed his tone.

"You'll be fine," he said. "I'll ask you a little bit about you and Eric's relationship when you were a judge. You can explain the pay voucher issue . . . and . . . uhh."

I could sense he was running back over the standard questions you ask a witness.

"But I will probably start with background questions about you, Aaron, the kids," he said, continuing. "Do your kids live at home?"

"Yes, they both did then," I said. "Now one is in college."

He spoke before he considered the real weight of his words, I think.

"Even better," he said. "I didn't know the ages of your kids."

Like most lawyers, he was absently commenting on how badly things could have gone, and thinking aloud about how much better it would sound to a jury. It was no consolation that I professionally understood what he meant, because now I was a potential target.

He must have figured out what my silence meant.

"You know what I mean," he said. "It's even better to show that since he wanted to kill you, which we know from Kim that he did, and that he would have killed everyone in the house. I won't ask you that. We will argue that." He meant that he wouldn't ask me the question directly, but that in closing arguments he would point out to the jury the potential carnage that could have happened at my home—with me, Aaron, Brad, and Jacob.

He knew that I understood. I had had these conversations with witnesses a hundred times during the years, preparing for trial. So without him saying it, I knew he meant for me to just answer the questions, not to volunteer anything and he would pull it all together in his closing arguments.

Shook said a few more things, reminded me to not watch the coverage, and wished me a good weekend. He hung up promising to call next week to let me know what day I would testify during the punishment hearing.

I held my office phone in my hand. I reached to hang it up and realized my hand was shaking.

This wasn't something that someone was talking about hypothetically anymore. This was really happening.

Chapter 24
I'm a Witness

THE SECOND WEEK of the Eric Williams trial proved very busy, both at home and at work. Thankfully, now that Eric had been convicted, the DA's office employees' interest had waned somewhat. That meant my staff had ramped back up to full swing, getting legal work done. At home, my son Brad had finished up fall term and had come home for Christmas. We were getting the house ready for the holidays.

I knew I was not supposed to talk to anyone about the case and I didn't.

My quarantine did not stop the swirl of sentiments that felt palpable in the courthouse hallways. Attorneys, who knew the defendant, were picking sides. Some felt he deserved lethal injection while others believed the ultimate price was too high.

Later, when I learned that some of the other attorneys still supported Eric Williams, it was disturbing. Deeply. They reasoned that Eric Williams was an attorney, after all. He was one of us. He had skills. But for his lapse in judgment in killing three people and plotting to kill more, he was really a good guy that got pushed into these murders because of the conviction by the prosecutors in the theft case. Some people still didn't believe he did it. Somehow their logic didn't make sense to me.

All week long, the State had put on its punishment evidence with witnesses in the penalty phase of trial. As the week came to a close, the state rested and it was the defense's turn. Even though the defense did not have to put on any evidence, the stakes were high. The defense mounted a vigorous defense and the drone of defense witnesses testifying continued. The public defenders called everyone: Williams's Boy Scout troop leader, his high school girlfriend, and more recently the attorneys that worked with him.

I began to think, since the week was ending, that Shook had decided not to call me after all. So, imagine my surprise when one week after his first call, Shook called me again.

It was Friday. This time he called me on my cell phone. I had programmed his number in, so I knew it was him when I answered the phone.

"What's up, Toby?" I asked.

"Oh, I think the defense is finishing up today or Monday at the latest," he said. "I just wanted you to know that I still intend on calling you. I'm calling you after another witness and then we will be done."

"You are calling me as a rebuttal witness?" I asked.

Rebuttal was the opportunity for the State (and the defense) to call witnesses to rebut the testimony in their opponent's case-in-chief. I had to admire the State's strategy that they had waited to call witnesses in rebuttal; Wirskye and Shook were true trial tacticians.

"Yes. After I call another witness."

He had used that phrase twice: "after another witness." I decided not to ask who it was or what that meant, because he was being mysterious and also it wasn't allowed to discuss what the other witnesses' testimony would be.

"Okay," I said. "Tuesday works."

"Good," he said. "I want you there early. I'd like to go over a few things with you before you get on the stand. You will be fine."

And for the second Friday in a row, he encouraged me to have a good weekend. I knew that until this case was over, my weekends were not going to be good. Thankfully, it looked like this would be the last restless weekend. The trial would be over soon.

A jury finding Williams guilty and seven days of punishment evidence made a big difference to my state of mind. This week, when I hit the red disconnect button on my phone, my hands were not shaking. Progress.

Still, anxiety crept in.

I went back over our conversation and got stuck on the phrase he had used twice: "after another witness." He had avoided telling me who the other witness was, but it had to be Kim Williams, the defendant's wife.

The prosecutors had not called her yet in either guilt or punishment to testify about her husband's diabolical plans. It was as if they were saving their best witnesses for last.

Kim Williams had cooperated with the prosecution. She had told investigators that after her husband killed Mike, the pair had celebrated with a steak dinner and an evening drive to Lake Tawakoni, where they tossed the mask that Eric had worn and the gun he used to murder Hasse.

Although her cooperation had led prosecutors to important evidence in the trial, I sensed that her greatest contribution had not happened yet. She was going to tie all the pieces together. Her testimony would also illustrate that the killing spree would have gone on and on, if not for his capture. There were more targets on his hit list.

Stop thinking and go home, Erleigh.

I got myself together and prepared to leave the office for the weekend. I double-checked my emails, phone messages, and my constant to-do list, and packed my brief bags with the work I needed to review over the weekend. I glanced back over the to-do list. There was no need to write "testify in Williams' trial" on my list. I was not likely to forget that item. The knot in my chest was reminder enough.

THE FOLLOWING TUESDAY, Chief Investigator Mike Holley came to my home to pick me up and escort me to the courthouse. Holley had been at most of the court proceedings, making himself available to assist with the victims or to perform any task that arose. As he drove me and my family over, I was reminded what an asset he was to the office and how fortunate I was to have hired him. Holley was capable, friendly, and managed to be everywhere at once. On top of that, he had a sense of humor.

Aaron and Brad rode over with us to the court hearing. They both wanted to support me during my testimony. Holley knew better than to talk to us about the facts of the case. We made idle conversation as he navigated from Forney to Rockwall, which was about a twenty-minute drive from our home.

Rockwall County had a new courthouse. You could see it from Interstate 30, the highway that connects Rockwall to Dallas across Lake Ray Hubbard. Referred to as the "mini-capitol" for its resemblance to our nation and state's capitol buildings, it was quite a sight to see on that Tuesday as we pulled up and parked.

Even though our county had one of the more infamous capital murder trials in the state, I had been to the courthouse only once during the proceedings. Today marked my second visit.

We made our way into the building and rode up the elevator. Holley greeted Rockwall County sheriff's deputies, who manned the magnetometers—the metal scanners used for security on the first floor—and showed us to the witness room, an area outside the courtroom. My family and I sat in the small witness room around a table with four chairs.

"Judge, I'm going to let Toby know you're here," Holley said. "I'll be right back."

Aaron reached out and grabbed my hand.

"You okay?" he asked.

"Yes," I said.

I looked at my son. His eyes were big as saucers. I knew Brad was old enough to understand the danger we had all been in April of 2013, but I don't think he totally appreciated how real that danger had been until now.

A trial makes everything more real. The fact that his mother had to testify emphasized that to him. I was going to ask Brad how he felt, but Holley interrupted by knocking on the door.

"I let Toby know you are here," he said, glancing at his watch and then back at me.

"Mike, go on in," I said. "There is no reason to stay here. Brad, you and Aaron, too. You are not 'under the rule.' Could be interesting."

Brad stood up.

"I will take him in with me," Holley said. "Let's go before they close the courtroom door."

I looked at Aaron, who was still sitting down.

"Go on in," I told him.

"No," he said. "I would rather sit here with you."

"It'll be boring," I said.

"Then I'll be bored," he said. "I've got my phone."

He held his iPhone in the air like a small trophy, as proof.

"Okay guys, go on," I said, smiling at Holley and Brad. "We are fine."

I tapped my watch, indicating that it was almost nine. Judge Snipes, as the presiding judge in the trial, had made it clear he did not want people interrupting while court was in session and the bailiffs followed his instructions. Once the trial started for that session, there was no coming in and out of the courtroom until the court recessed.

I did not know how long I was going to have to sit in the witness room before I was called or even if I would be called. I knew sometimes things changed, and the attorneys might decide they didn't need me. I had brought work, iPad, and my phone, and so had planned on answering emails, working on some office matters, and doing some online Christmas shopping.

Time passed.

At some point, I realized I was staring at the same email because my brain had finally caught up to what was happening. It would no longer let me act as if the routine occurrences of my life could minimize the significance of this moment.

I, Erleigh Wiley, sat in a witness room not as a lawyer, but as a target of a crime. Not just any crime, but murder.

Eric Williams, my would-be killer, sat not far from me in the next room, on trial for killing three people. Later today, the jurors would know that he was a man who would have killed again.

Not some random person. Not a stranger.

Me.

Another knock cut through my reverie.

"Come in," Aaron and I answered in unison.

In walked Toby Shook, dressed in a dark single-button suit, white shirt, and red tie. He looked every bit a prosecutor. He held a yellow legal pad and looked in charge, confident.

Things must be going well in court.

He shook Aaron's hand and looked directly at me.

"We're on a recess," he said. "You are up next. Kim just finished testifying."

Aaron got up and walked out of the room, shutting the door behind him. Aaron knew that Shook would want to go over some of my testimony with me alone.

"I want you to remember to listen to what I ask you," he said. "You are used to asking questions, but you're answering them today. I'm going to walk you through the testimony we talked about on the phone: the pay sheets, him getting off the appointment list and then getting back on, who lived at your home with you last year when these murders happened."

He paused to really look at me.

"Are you with me?" he asked. "Are you okay?"

"Sure, I'm fine," I said. "Just a little nervous."

"That's expected," he said.

He smiled and went back to where he was with my trial prep.

"I'm going to start with some general question: background, family, role as wife and mother," he said. "Any questions?"

Toby stood up, signaling the end of our conversation.

"No, I've got it," I said.

"Stay in here," he said. "Someone will come get you, when we call you. See you in there."

After he left, Aaron came back in.

"I want to go sit in the courtroom now, so I won't get locked out when you start your testimony," he said. "You okay?"

"I'm fine," I said, trying to reassure us both.

"You look fine," he teased. He gave me a warm hug and walked out.

I was alone in the witness room. I had nothing else to do but wait.

"STATE YOUR NAME, for the record," Shook said, as he began my direct testimony.

I had asked that question myself many times to witnesses throughout the years, first as an ADA and later as a judge. It really wasn't a question at all, but a statement. It was the starting point for any attorney with his witness, an easy way to introduce the jury to the witness, and make clear on the record the identity of the person testifying.

"Judge Wiley, where do you reside?" Shook asked. "Not your exact address, but what county?"

I glanced around the room. First, I looked up to my left where the judge sat on the bench. Judge Snipes was leaning a little forward toward the witness stand where I was sitting. He looked steadily at me and over my head at the jury, his gaze neither encouraging nor discouraging. I thought he had the right practiced effect for a judge.

Judge Snipes had been appointed as a visiting judge in this case when Judge Chitty recused himself. Judge Chitty had been the judge that presided over the Williams theft case and was a witness in the capital murder trial. Snipes's reputation preceded him. He had been a hard-hitting federal prosecutor and a state judge hearing difficult cases. He was the right fit for this case.

As I spoke, I looked to my right, toward the twelve jurors. I saw that they were paying attention and leaning in. That was a good sign.

"Tell us a little bit about your family, your kids," Shook said, following up.

I glanced at him and the other members of the trial team. I realized he was trying to get me to relax and provide background information for the jury and the record. I looked to the left of where Toby sat and there was Eric Williams and his trial team at the other set of tables, occupied by the defendant and his team of lawyers.

Eric Williams wore a suit, white shirt, and a tie, dressed as I had seen him many times before in court or around the courthouse. Dressed the same as when he represented defendants, before he decided to join their criminal ranks. Today, even though he looked the same, he sat there convicted of capital murder for killing three people and wanted me among the dead.

He would not look at me. He looked down as I testified.

"So, Judge, explain for the jury, how it was that you had contact with Eric Williams?" Shook asked.

I looked back at Shook and took a breath, which helped to even the sound of my voice. It had been tiny before. I answered his questions and we moved through the direct examination: question, answer, question, answer.

We established for the jury that Eric Williams seemed like any other attorney. He had an office around the courthouse square, which was dotted with office space, eateries, and small businesses. He primarily represented children and served as their attorney ad litem in cases when they had been removed from their parents. I told the twelve of them that until I was asked to review his pay sheets—documents that the other judges, commissioners, and the auditor had felt were unusually excessive —he and I had a friendly, professional relationship.

I also told them that after I confronted him about the pay discrepancies, he wasn't happy about me questioning him. It didn't seem to matter that the amounts of the invoices he submitted were close to half a million dollars in three years. After I questioned him, he requested to be removed from the list of attorneys that did that kind of work, even though I had never requested his removal.

Eric Williams loathed me and planned to kill me because I had the audacity to question him. In his warped mind, I was the beginning of his end. His deadly hit list had taken seed between my confrontation of his illegal behavior and Mike McLelland and Mark Hasse's prosecution of his criminal theft case.

Even though he refused to look at me, I felt better. In fact, I felt better than I had imagined I would have now that I had an opportunity to confront Eric Williams with my testimony in court.

His evil plan would never make sense to a rational person, but I knew that the prosecution team had done a good job in dissecting his maniacal mind. He had been wronged, whether real or imagined, and his solution was to kill the wrongdoers.

It was so beyond anything you could imagine. So many easier solutions existed that would have been able to prevent all of this from happening. Eric could have decided to do some other type of legal work. He could have stopped overbilling the county and simply continued the legal work he was doing. He could have decided to not steal computer equipment from the county, or once caught, he could have taken a plea deal and saved his Texas bar license; and ultimately he could have moved to another town to practice and start over. How many times had I thought about scenarios, said these words aloud, and now I had said them to the ultimate decision makers—the jury. None of these were options anymore for Eric Williams.

The cross-examination by Matthew Seymour, Williams's lawyer, was brief and then it was over; finally, it was blessedly over.

I looked at the jurors. Some of the women had tears in their eyes. They knew this guy would have killed me and my family. They believed me. They were smarter than me in that they grasped the facts the first time. It had taken me too long to accept that I was next on the list.

It was only later that I realized that Kim Williams's chilling testimony had set the scene for mine. Her deadly predictions of future murders from her husband's hit list came to life when the jury got to hear testimony from me, one of the next victims on the killer's list—his next target.

| PART FOUR |

Chapter 25
The Trial: 20/20 Hindsight

BEING CALLED AS a witness in the trial meant I was placed under "the Rule," which, in legal terms, means that you are sworn in as a witness, and that you swear or affirm that you will not listen to or speak to anyone, except the attorneys involved in the case. I took the Rule seriously and did not listen to the testimony or discuss the testimony with any of the witnesses in the case, but later I did research the trial and discuss the case with attorneys, investigators, officers, family members of the victims, and friends. I knew the murders were horrific, but that Eric Williams wanted to send a message with these murders. As I went back through the details of the murders, it was chilling. We know that in this life, we will all die eventually, but a murder is different. A murderer takes everything away from you and your family, senselessly and, in this case, viciously. Murder is the quintessential assaultive crime, but it is a theft too. In fact, it is the worst theft of all, stealing a human life, the ending of their future, and the taking of a family's joy because of the loss of their loved one. The following are some of my observations of the murders after learning the facts.

Mark

Mark Hasse was the type of man who, upon first observation, seemed nondescript. He had a slight build, and was an average-looking, non-threatening, bespectacled man, but when he opened his mouth, all of that changed. When he talked about the law, he lit up, becoming engaged and full of life. He had a thirty-year repertoire of stories from criminal cases he had reviewed, negotiated, and tried as a prosecutor, special prosecutor, or defense attorney. The good part was that his stories weren't just lawyer lies—they were true. He took his job seriously.

Mark liked order and he operated his life in an efficient and precise manner. His favorite hobby, aviation, had honed that skill within him. Mark arrived at work on the morning of January 30, 2013. He pulled his car into the county parking lot around 8:30 a.m. He parked his car in the same location at the same time every morning he went to work. He got out of his vehicle, clicking the lock and grabbing his brief case. His briefcase contained work documents, but just as importantly, he had his firearm in his bag. Mark made no secret of carrying a gun. He was a certified peace officer and an ADA, so he had a legal right to carry. He also knew that with a thirty-year history of prosecuting bad people, some of them might want him dead. But that morning, he never got a chance to retrieve his gun from his briefcase.

His assailant was masked, wearing a bulletproof vest, dressed in dark clothes and Army boots. He confronted Mark once he got out of the car. Their exchange was brief, but it was clear they knew each other. Mark uttered the words, "I'm sorry, I'm sorry." There was no mercy in the killer. He raised his arm and shot Mark at point blank range in the chest and finished the job, standing over him; shooting him in the neck, as Mark lay dying in the parking lot. Gunshots rang into the air as the shooter retrieved another gun, all the while pumping the trigger rapidly. The additional gunfire was necessary to keep the crowd at bay (and any would-be witnesses), as the killer got into his car and drove away.

A good Samaritan and then an officer that was first to the scene worked on Mark, giving him chest compressions and mouth-to-mouth, hoping to resuscitate him, as they waited on the ambulance to arrive—to no avail.

The murder was efficient, cold, planned, and daring. Mark was killed in the county parking lot, only yards away from the courthouse. Police vehicles moved around the courthouse square seeking parking places, while citizens hustled to the courthouse attending to their legal affairs; the murderer calmly got into his car and drove away from the crime scene undetected.

The trail had run cold on Mark's murder, but the killer was not done. He struck again on March 31, 2013.

Mike

A man's home is his castle. It's a common saying that epitomizes an understanding of the sanctity of your home. Where you live is important and cherished, since it's a place that you want to go to be safe.

If you were ever around Mike and Cynthia McLelland, you knew that they were a couple that was still very much in love. They were a mature couple, but their fondness for each other was not dimmed by their years. They enjoyed separate hobbies. Cynthia loved quilting; Mike was a former military man and amateur military historian. They had purchased a newer home for entertaining and had moved from nearby Terrell to Forney, a larger, more sprawling residence. They were proud of their new home purchase.

When the slaughter began at the residence on Blarney Stone Way, the door was unlocked, there was no indication of forced entry, and Cynthia was near the front door. She was clad in only a night shirt, but I believe she trusted the man who appeared to be a deputy on the other side of the door's entrance. Turning on the porch light, and cracking the door a smidge to ask the officer to wait while they dressed, the door was forced open. The killer pushed her back from the entryway and shot Cynthia. The trajectory of the shot traveled throughout her body, causing damage in its wake.

That morning Mike was clad only in sweats and flip-flops. It seemed that after he heard the gunfire, he went for his cache of weapons that had been safely put away because of an Easter egg hunt later that day with small children. He never made it to his firepower; his body was riddled with gunshot wounds.

There were over twenty shots that were fired in the home and they knew that the carnage took two minutes because of a timer that was attached to a burglar alarm at the home. The alarm had been purchased and installation started two months earlier after Mark was killed, but the alarm system installation was never completed.

As the murderer exited the residence, he thought his carnage was complete, until Cynthia moaned. Her assailant unmercifully shot her as she clung to life, exiting their home at 6:42 a.m. The killer had expressed to his wife that Cynthia was collateral damage and he couldn't leave a witness behind. Like Mark's crime scene, the assailant calmly got into his vehicle and drove away. No one stopped him. There was no encounter. No one heard the gunshots and called the police. There was no chase that ensued. The killer thought as he did before he had gotten away with murder again. His plan was to continue down his list . . . he had other targets to hit.

Epilogue

IN THE MIDST of the everyday rhythm of life, these murders came to my community and to me, unplanned and unexpected. No one expects to be the target of a murder plot, particularly by a former colleague.

After all the years of being around the criminal element, this situation taught me one important lesson: don't be fooled by the well-dressed and well-heeled educated criminal.

Eric Williams had taken entitlement to a new level. He proved far more deadly than the average street-level criminal. Eric Williams and his ilk can be easily overlooked as a danger.

The good news is that psychopaths like Eric Williams are a very small part of our population. And like most criminals, they make mistakes. Eric Williams's mistakes came with his crime stopper tip that he couldn't resist making and the contents of his storage unit, which contained his evil tools. The now famous Unit 18 in Seagoville, which contained the getaway vehicle: a white Crown Ford Victoria. Besides the getaway vehicle, there were weapons and a single unspent shell casing, effectively tying the crime scenes together with one weapon.

It became even more evident to me as the months after the trial unfolded, as we made through Christmas, New Year's, and Valentine's Day, that I had been fortunate to miss my brush with this evil psychopath who had created so much havoc in the lives of the McLelland and Hasse families and the citizens of Kaufman County.

Then, in late February, the Williams trial team set a motion for new trial hearing in front of the court, based upon newly discovered evidence, namely brain scans that had been performed on Williams. The defense asserted that Judge Snipes would not grant a continuance during the trial to allow for this type of testing. Further, if the jury had heard the evidence, the defense argued that the jury would not have imposed the death penalty because the scans showed he had a broken brain.

They were wrong.

I had mistakenly thought that by the time I testified against Eric Williams, he was a broken man. That perhaps as he sat in the courtroom with his head bowed, he was contrite for the sufferings of the families that had lost loved ones at his hands. I assumed his bowed head signified compliance, contrition, defeat.

I was wrong, too.

It was an act. He felt none of those emotions. That became clear at the motion for new trial hearing.

Once there, Eric Williams did not want to remain in the courtroom. So after the judge questioned him and was assured he understood he had a right to be in the courtroom during the proceedings, Eric Williams was allowed to leave under armed guard after he insisted that he wanted to leave.

Unbeknownst to anyone, I was walking down an empty hallway heading toward one of the court offices after the judge's admonishment. Flanked by two deputies, one on each side, Eric Williams walked toward the exit door and the waiting squad car to go back to the county jail.

In that moment, I locked eyes with Eric Williams.

His head was not bowed. His spirit was not broken. He passed me without a word. He never flinched, wavered, or looked away.

Although Eric said nothing, he glared at me all the way down the hall. Squinting and narrowing his gaze at me, his eyes dared me to look away. I didn't. The two deputies hustled him by as fast as they could propel his shackled feet.

Once he passed me, he never looked back.

Those few seconds were one of the most uncomfortable moments of my life. I exhaled when he passed and headed out the door. It had been unnerving.

I knew in those moments that I never wanted that man out of prison. I knew he felt that his work was not done. He had left unfinished business.

And I was it.

ARE WE AT a time in history when we can't work out our differences? Have we forgotten that freedom means that we are meant to solve our disagreements through discourse and not violence? Ultimately, Eric Williams could not handle the outcomes of his decisions. The decision to overbill the county; the decision to steal computer equipment from the county; the decision to not accept responsibility when the jury found him guilty; and the final decision to take innocent lives.

Are people like Williams evil? If he was in fact evil, then can you ever overcome evil? I truly believe that putting light into the darkness is the only way to overcome fear.

Fear is real . . . it can temporarily paralyze the senses, or leave your heart pounding uncontrollably, altering the way you breath. It's very real.

We all have fears and anxieties. It can be a new job, changing cities, or simply introducing yourself to strangers. It may be small or large, but overcoming that tension as we move through our lives is a goal that every person wants to achieve.

I was raised as the only girl in a family of four brothers. I had a strong mother, and a father who was never intimated by my mom's strength. He was a social trailblazer, committed to supporting the women in his life. This passed down through the generations of my family, my father's strong mother, then my mother, and then me.

My parents believed that their children could accomplish anything. And they instilled that belief in us as we grew up. It didn't matter that I was a girl—that just made my mother push harder. Sometimes when I doubt what I should do, I think of my mother and I wonder what she would do. And no matter how difficult the task is before me, I always know that the accomplishments she and her contemporaries achieved in their time were much greater than the tasks before me.

As the murders in 2013 unraveled and the investigation hung in the balance, I decided to make a leap of faith, not because I'm brave, but because I knew it was the right thing to do. I stood at the crossroads, not just of my career, but of my life. So I stepped up, just like so many people every day step up to the challenges that are before them. The fear I felt then is no different than the anxieties that other people have as they make difficult decisions, but, like all anxieties about our choices, acting is the hardest part.

After I accepted the appointment as DA, I never questioned the decision again. The DA position is where I am supposed to be and it is where I have remained since the appointment. My children are no longer teenagers, but college-age men fulfilling their own lives. My husband continues to thrive. He left the government and is a partner in a law firm in the private sector. He still likes to tell me when he thinks he is right; sometimes I listen, sometimes I don't.

Over fifty years ago, I was born in Kaufman County, and I have lived there most of my life. A killer came to Kaufman County, and hunted people that he thought wronged him. He is gone now, but my county and I survived.

Acknowledgments

I am grateful to the many people who assisted me with this book. It started with a story recounting the terrible events that happened in Kaufman County. One night over dinner, friends, Steve and Vanesa Odell said that the story was captivating and that it needed to be a book. From there the project went from an idea to a reality. Additionally, without the editing help of Jade Mens, this memoir may have, quite possibly, gone nowhere. Many experienced authors lent their time and knowledge, particularly Victor McGlothin, who with Shelton Gibbs, who lent time and much advice. My agent, Leticia Gomez guided me through this process. And the staff of Skyhorse Publishing who enabled me to publish this book.

Having the courage and time to put your thoughts to paper requires an extensive support system. My sons, Joseph (Brad) and Jacob have encouraged me throughout this process. To my aunt, Hester Fletcher (auntie), who read my first draft and gave me suggestions about the book. To biggest fan and husband, Aaron, who listened, critiqued, and made the journey of writing this book alongside me. Truly, there would not have been a book without him.

My undying thanks go to the men and women that protect our country daily; particularly those on our detail from Immigration Custom Enforcement-Homeland in 2013. They gave up their time with their families, to protect mine. And to the men and women that worked tirelessly on solving the case, gathering the evidence, and prosecuting the case; my gratitude and appreciation knows no bound. The prosecution team was led by Bill Wirskye, Toby Shook, and Jeri Sims. Local, state, and federal agencies worked together under the direction of Sheriff David Byrnes, processing volumes of evidence that lead to an unprecedented victory for the prosecution.

The families of the slain can never be forgotten. I may have been on the hit list, but they lost their loved ones. I have had the privilege of meeting many of their family and friends and I know they will be forever missed. I give special honor to all victims of crime, but particularly to the families of Mark, Mike and Cynthia.

On behalf of myself, my office, and the community of Kaufman County, we appreciate the outpouring of support after the horrific events that happened in Kaufman County. There was unwavering support from county and district attorney offices throughout the state and the nation, particularly the Texas District County Attorney's Association.

Without the support of my colleagues and the confidence of Governor's Perry office, I would never have been the Criminal District Attorney. Finally, a special thanks to the staff of County Court-at-Law, who supported me as I made the transition from judge to the Kaufman County District Attorney's Office. They never stopped doing their job.